Complete
SPOKEN ARABIC

For Adult Beginners

Speak Arabic In 30 Days

Dr Abdul Mughees
PhD in Arabic

I fondly dedicated this book to
my mother and father.

Contents

Preface	5
Chapter 1: Introductions and Greetings	7
Chapter 2: Talking About Nationality and Origin	11
Chapter 3: Family and Relationships	16
Chapter 4: Talking About Jobs and Occupations	20
Chapter 5: Daily Routines	24
Chapter 6: Ordering at a Restaurant	28
Chapter 7: Shopping and Prices	33
Chapter 8: Describing People and Personalities	38
Chapter 9: Talking About Hobbies and Free Time	43
Chapter 10: Asking for Directions	48
Chapter 11: Travel and Airports	52
Chapter 12: Health and Visiting a Doctor	57
Chapter 13: Weather and Seasons	62
Chapter 14: Time and Dates	67
Chapter 15: Expressing Opinions and Preferences	72
Chapter 16: Talking About Places and Directions	77
Chapter 17: Making and Cancelling Plans	81
Chapter 18: Asking for Help and Assistance	86
Chapter 19: Social Media and Technology	90
Chapter 20: Describing Objects	95
Chapter 21: At the Hotel	100
Chapter 22: Renting a House or Apartment	104
Chapter 23: Talking About the Past	109
Chapter 24: Future Plans and Goals	115
Chapter 25: Discussing Education and Schools	120
Chapter 26: Talking About Transportation	125
Chapter 27: Cultural Traditions and Celebrations	130
Chapter 28: Business Arabic	135

Preface

Learning a new language is like embarking on an exciting journey—a journey that not only expands your communication skills but also opens doors to new cultures, perspectives, and connections. Whether you're learning Arabic for travel, work, or personal enrichment, this book, **"Complete Spoken Arabic For Adult Beginners: Speak Arabic In 30 Days"** is designed to guide you every step of the way.

As the author of this book, I remember my own experiences with language learning—how overwhelming it felt at first, yet how rewarding it became with every new word and conversation. I wanted to create a resource that would make the process as smooth and enjoyable as possible for new learners, and that's how this 30-day course came to life.

Arabic is spoken by millions of people across the world, from bustling markets in Morocco to the vibrant streets of Dubai. It's a language rich in history, culture, and beauty. Learning Arabic gives you the chance to connect more deeply with the Arab world, appreciate its traditions, and engage with people on a personal level.

This book is not just a collection of phrases or vocabulary lists; it's a carefully structured course designed to build your confidence and get you speaking Arabic from day one. Each chapter focuses on a real-life topic—whether it's introducing yourself, ordering food at a restaurant, or talking about your daily routine. The dialogues are practical and relatable, and the accompanying exercises are crafted to reinforce your learning in a way that feels natural.

Over the next 30 days, you will dive into everyday conversations that cover a wide range of topics. The dialogues are simple yet authentic, reflecting how Arabic is actually spoken in daily life. Each chapter introduces new vocabulary, pronunciation guides, and translations to help you understand the context and meaning behind each sentence. This book is designed to be accessible to everyone, whether you're a complete beginner or looking to improve your conversational skills.

I understand the challenges that come with learning a new language, especially one as distinct and beautiful as Arabic. There might be moments when you feel stuck, frustrated, or unsure of your progress. In those times, remember why you started. Think of the connections you'll make, the cultures you'll better understand, and the confidence you'll gain in using Arabic in real-world situations. Learning Arabic is not just about mastering words and phrases; it's about building bridges between people and cultures.

I hope this book becomes more than just a learning tool—I hope it inspires you, challenges you, and ultimately helps you achieve your goal of speaking Arabic with confidence.

So, grab a cup of tea, find a quiet spot, and let's begin this journey together. Thank you for choosing this book and I look forward to seeing you succeed in your Arabic learning adventure!

Author
Dr Abdul Mughees
PhD in Arabic

Chapter 1

Basic Greetings and Introductions

Key Vocabulary:

Arabic	Pronunciation	Translation
مرحبًا	Marḥaban	Hello
صباح الخير	Ṣabāḥ al-khayr	Good morning
مساء الخير	Masā' al-khayr	Good evening
كيف حالك؟	Kayfa ḥāluka (m) / ḥāluki (f)	How are you? (m/f)
بخير	Bikhayr	I'm fine
شكرًا	Shukran	Thank you
اسمي	Ismī	My name is
من أين أنت؟	Min ayna anta (m) / anti (f)?	Where are you from? (m/f)
أنا من	Anā min	I am from
سررت بلقائك	Surirtu biliqā'ika (m) / biliqā'iki (f)	Nice to meet you (m/f)

Dialogue 1: Informal Greetings

Scenario: You meet someone for the first time at a café. It's a casual setting, and you greet them informally.

Arabic: مرحبًا، كيف حالك؟
Pronunciation: Marḥaban, kayfa ḥāluka?
Translation: Hello, how are you?

Arabic: أنا بخير، شكرًا. كيف حالك أنت؟
Pronunciation: Anā bikhayr, shukran. Kayfa ḥāluka anta?
Translation: I'm fine, thank you. How are you?

Arabic: أنا بخير أيضًا.
Pronunciation: Anā bikhayr ayḍan.
Translation: I'm fine as well.

Arabic: ما اسمك؟
Pronunciation: Mā ismuka?
Translation: What's your name?

Arabic: اسمي أحمد. وأنت؟
Pronunciation: Ismī Aḥmad. Wa anta?
Translation: My name is Ahmad. And you?

Arabic: اسمي علي.
Pronunciation: Ismī ʿAlī.
Translation: My name is Ali.

Dialogue 2: Formal Introductions

Scenario: You are meeting a colleague for the first time at a formal event.

Arabic: صباح الخير. كيف حالك؟
Pronunciation: Ṣabāḥ al-khayr. Kayfa ḥāluka?
Translation: Good morning. How are you?

Arabic: بخير، شكرًا. وأنت؟
Pronunciation: Bikhayr, shukran. Wa anta?
Translation: I'm fine, thank you. And you?

Arabic: بخير، الحمد لله.
Pronunciation: Bikhayr, al-ḥamdu lillāh.
Translation: I'm fine, praise be to God.

Arabic: اسمي سارة. سررت بلقائك.
Pronunciation: Ismī Sārah. Surirtu biliqā'ika.
Translation: My name is Sarah. Nice to meet you.

Arabic: سررت بلقائك أيضًا.
Pronunciation: Surirtu biliqā'ika ayḍan.
Translation: Nice to meet you too.

Dialogue 3: Asking Where Someone is From

Scenario: You are talking to a new friend and want to know where they are from.

Arabic: من أين أنت؟
Pronunciation: Min ayna anta (m) / anti (f)?
Translation: Where are you from?

Arabic: أنا من الهند. وأنت؟
Pronunciation: Anā min al-Hind. Wa anta?
Translation: I'm from India. And you?

Arabic: أنا من مصر.
Pronunciation: Anā min Miṣr.
Translation: I'm from Egypt.

Arabic: سررت بلقائك.
Pronunciation: Surirtu biliqā'ika.
Translation: Nice to meet you.

Arabic: سررت بلقائك أيضًا.
Pronunciation: Surirtu biliqā'ika ayḍan.
Translation: Nice to meet you too.

Exercise:

Translate the following sentences into Arabic

1. Hello, how are you?
2. Good morning! How are you today?
3. I'm fine, thank you. How are you?
4. My name is Ali. What is your name?
5. Nice to meet you.
6. I'm from India. Where are you from?
7. I'm fine as well. Thank you.
8. I am from Egypt.
9. Where are you from?
10. My name is Sarah. Nice to meet you.
11. Good evening! How are you?
12. I am from Morocco. Where are you from?
13. I'm fine, praise be to God.
14. What's your name?
15. Hello, I am Ahmad. Nice to meet you.
16. I'm from Saudi Arabia. And you?
17. Hello! My name is Youssef. How are you?
18. I'm fine, thank you. What about you?
19. Where are you from? I'm from Lebanon.
20. Nice to meet you too!

Chapter 2

Talking About Nationality and Origin

Key Vocabulary:

Arabic	Pronunciation	Translation
ما جنسيتك؟	Mā jinsīyatuka (m) / jinsīyatuki (f)?	What is your nationality? (m/f)
أنا من	Anā min	I am from
أنا هندي	Anā Hindī	I am Indian
أنت مصري	Anta (m) Miṣrī / Anti (f) Miṣrīyah	You are Egyptian (m/f)
فرنسي	Faransī	French (m)
فرنسية	Faransīyah	French (f)
أمريكي	Amrīkī	American (m)
أمريكية	Amrīkīyah	American (f)
سعودي	Saʿūdī	Saudi (m)
سعودية	Saʿūdīyah	Saudi (f)
بريطاني	Brīṭānī	British (m)
بريطانية	Brīṭānīyah	British (f)
من أي بلد أنت؟	Min ayy balad anta (m) / anti (f)?	From which country are you? (m/f)
بلد	Balad	Country
الجنسية	al-Jinsīyah	Nationality
عربي/عربية	Arabīyah/Arabi	Arab (f/m)

Dialogue 1: Asking About Nationality
Scenario: You meet someone at a conference and ask about their nationality.

Arabic: ما جنسيتك؟
Pronunciation: Mā jinsīyatuka?
Translation: What is your nationality?

Arabic: أنا هندي. وأنت؟
Pronunciation: Anā Hindī. Wa anta?
Translation: I am Indian. And you?

Arabic: أنا مصري. هل زرت الهند من قبل؟
Pronunciation: Anā Miṣrī. Hal zurta al-Hind min qablu?
Translation: I am Egyptian. Have you visited India before?

Arabic: نعم، زرت الهند مرة واحدة. بلد جميل!
Pronunciation: Naʿam, zurta al-Hind marrah wāḥidah. Balad jamīl!
Translation: Yes, I visited India once. It's a beautiful country!

Arabic: شكرًا! هل زرت مصر؟
Pronunciation: Shukran! Hal zurta Miṣr?
Translation: Thank you! Have you visited Egypt?

Arabic: لا، لكن أتمنى زيارة مصر يومًا ما.
Pronunciation: Lā, lakin atamanā ziyārat Miṣr yawman mā.
Translation: No, but I hope to visit Egypt someday.

Arabic: ستكون مرحبًا بك دائمًا في مصر.
Pronunciation: Satakūnu marḥaban bika dā’iman fī Miṣr.
Translation: You will always be welcome in Egypt.

Dialogue 2: Talking About Origin

Scenario: You are talking to a new friend about your country of origin.

Arabic: من أي بلد أنت؟
Pronunciation: Min ayy balad anta?
Translation: From which country are you?

Arabic: أنا من فرنسا. وأنت؟
Pronunciation: Anā min Faransā. Wa anta?
Translation: I’m from France. And you?

Arabic: أنا من السعودية. هل زرت فرنسا من قبل؟
Pronunciation: Anā min al-Saʿūdīyah. Hal zurta Faransā min qablu?
Translation: I’m from Saudi Arabia. Have you visited France before?

Arabic: نعم، زرت باريس في الصيف الماضي.
Pronunciation: Naʿam, zurta Bārīs fī aṣ-ṣayf al-māḍī.
Translation: Yes, I visited Paris last summer.

Arabic: رائع! ماذا أحببت في باريس؟
Pronunciation: Rā’iʿ! Mādhā aḥbabta fī Bārīs?
Translation: Wonderful! What did you like about Paris?

Arabic: أحببت المعالم السياحية والطعام الفرنسي.
Pronunciation: Aḥbabtu al-maʿālim as-siyāḥīyah wa aṭ-ṭaʿām al-Faransī.
Translation: I liked the tourist attractions and the French food.

Arabic: هذا جميل! أتمنى زيارة باريس قريبًا.
Pronunciation: Hādhā jamīl! Atamanā ziyārat Bārīs qarīban.
Translation: That's great! I hope to visit Paris soon.

Arabic: ستكون تجربة رائعة. باريس مدينة رائعة!
Pronunciation: Satakūnu tajribah rā'iʿah. Bārīs madīnah rā'iʿah!
Translation: It will be a wonderful experience. Paris is a beautiful city!

Dialogue 3: Describing Nationalities

Scenario: You are at an international meeting and people are talking about their nationalities.

Arabic: أنت أمريكي؟
Pronunciation: Anta Amrīkī?
Translation: Are you American?

Arabic: نعم، أنا أمريكي. وأنت؟
Pronunciation: Naʿam, anā Amrīkī. Wa anta?
Translation: Yes, I am American. And you?

Arabic: أنا بريطاني.
Pronunciation: Anā Brīṭānī.
Translation: I am British.

Arabic: هل أنت عربية؟
Pronunciation: Hal anti ʿArabīyah?
Translation: Are you Arab? (f)

Arabic: نعم، أنا عربية.
Pronunciation: Naʿam, anā ʿArabīyah.
Translation: Yes, I am Arab.

Exercise:

Translate the following sentences into Arabic

1. What is your nationality?
2. I am from India. Where are you from?
3. I am French. And you?
4. Are you Egyptian?
5. Yes, I am Egyptian.
6. He is from Saudi Arabia.
7. She is American.
8. Where are you from?
9. I am from Morocco.
10. My friend is British.
11. Is she from France?
12. He is not American.
13. My nationality is Indian.
14. What nationality are you?
15. I am from Saudi Arabia.
16. Are you from Morocco?
17. She is not French.
18. We are from Egypt.
19. I am not from America.
20. He is Saudi, but I am British.

Chapter 3

Family and Relationships

Key Vocabulary:

Arabic	Pronunciation	Translation
عائلة	ʿĀ'ilah	Family
والد	Wālid	Father
والدة	Wālidah	Mother
أخ	Akh	Brother
أخت	Ukht	Sister
ابن	Ib'n	Son
ابنة	Ibnah	Daughter
جد	Jadd	Grandfather
جدة	Jaddah	Grandmother
عم	ʿAmm	Uncle
عمة	ʿAmmih	Aunt
ابن عم	Ibn ʿAmm	Cousin (male)
ابنة عم	Bint ʿAmm	Cousin (female)
زوج	Zawj	Husband
زوجة	Zawjah	Wife
نحن	Naḥnu	We
عائلتي	ʿĀ'ilatī	My family
كم فرد في عائلتك؟	Kam fard fī ʿā'ilatika?	How many members are in your family?
لدينا	Ladaynā	We have
أعيش مع	ʿĀ'īsh maʿ	I live with

Dialogue 1: Introducing Family Members

Scenario: You are meeting a new friend and introducing your family.

Arabic: عائلتي كبيرة. لدينا خمسة أفراد.
Pronunciation: ʿĀ'ilatī kabīrah. Ladaynā khamsah afrād.
Translation: My family is large. We have five members.

Arabic: من هم أفراد عائلتك؟
Pronunciation: Min hum afrād ʿā'ilatika?
Translation: Who are the members of your family?

Arabic: والدي ووالدتي، وأخي، وأختي، وأنا.
Pronunciation: Wālidī wa wālidatī, wa akhī, wa ukhtī, wa anā.
Translation: My father, my mother, my brother, my sister, and I.

Dialogue 2: Discussing Family Relationships

Scenario: You are talking about your family relationships with a new acquaintance.

Arabic: كيف علاقتك مع والدك؟
Pronunciation: Kayfa ʿalāqtuka maʿ wālidika?
Translation: How is your relationship with your father?

Arabic: علاقتي مع والدي جيدة. هو يدعمني دائمًا.
Pronunciation: ʿAlāqtī maʿ wālidī jayyidah. Huwa yadʿumnī dā'iman.
Translation: My relationship with my father is good. He always supports me.

Arabic: وماذا عن والدتك؟
Pronunciation: Wa mādhā ʿan wālidatik?
Translation: And what about your mother?

Arabic: والدتي رائعة! تحب مساعدتي في الدراسة.
Pronunciation: Wālidatī rā'iʿah! Tuḥibb musāʿadatī fī ad-dirāsah.
Translation: My mother is wonderful! She loves to help me with my studies.

Dialogue 3: Talking About Siblings

Scenario: You are discussing your siblings and their roles in your life.

Arabic: هل لديك إخوة أو أخوات؟
Pronunciation: Hal ladayka ikhwa or akhawāt?
Translation: Do you have brothers or sisters?

Arabic: نعم، لدي أخ وأخت.
Pronunciation: Naʿam, ladayya akh wa ukht.
Translation: Yes, I have a brother and a sister.

Arabic: ماذا يفعل أخوك؟
Pronunciation: Mādhā yafʿal akhuka?
Translation: What does your brother do?

Arabic: أخي طالب في الجامعة.
Pronunciation: Akhī ṭālib fī al-jāmiʿah.
Translation: My brother is a student at university.

Arabic: وأختك، ماذا تفعل؟
Pronunciation: Wa ukhtuka, mādhā tafʿal?
Translation: And your sister, what does she do?

Arabic: أختي تعمل مدرسة.
Pronunciation: Ukhtī taʿmal mudarrisah.
Translation: My sister works as a teacher.

Exercise:

Translate the following sentences into Arabic

1. My family is large.
2. I have a father and a mother.
3. My brother is a student.
4. My sister is a teacher.
5. We live together as a family.
6. My grandfather is very wise.
7. My grandmother loves to cook.
8. I have one brother and one sister.
9. My aunt is visiting us this week.
10. My uncle works in a bank.
11. My cousin is younger than me.
12. We are a close family.
13. How many members are in your family?
14. I love my family very much.
15. My parents support me in my studies.
16. My brother plays football every weekend.
17. My sister enjoys painting.
18. My father has a good job.
19. My mother takes care of the house.
20. I often spend time with my cousins.

Chapter 4

Talking About Jobs and Occupations

Key Vocabulary:

Arabic	Pronunciation	Translation
وظيفة	Waẓīfah	Job
مهنة	Mihnah	Profession/Occupation
يعمل	Yaʿmal	He works
أعمل	Aʿmal	I work
طبيب	Ṭabīb	Doctor
مهندس	Muhandis	Engineer
معلم	Muʿallim	Teacher
مدير	Mudīr	Manager
محاسب	Muḥāsib	Accountant
محامي	Muḥāmī	Lawyer
سائق	Sā'iq	Driver
ممرض	Mumariḍ	Nurse
شرطي	Shurṭī	Police officer
طباخ	Ṭabbākh	Cook/Chef
عامل	ʿĀmil	Worker
مبرمج	Mubarrim	Programmer
وظيفة	Waẓīfah	Job
يعمل في	Yaʿmal fī	He works in
شركة	Sharikah	Company
مستشفى	Mustashfā	Hospital

Dialogue 1: Asking About Jobs

Scenario: You are meeting someone for the first time and want to ask about their job.

Arabic: ماذا تعمل؟
Pronunciation: Mādhā taʿmal?
Translation: What do you do for a living?

Arabic: أنا طبيب. وأنت؟
Pronunciation: Anā ṭabīb. Wa anta?
Translation: I am a doctor. And you?

Arabic: أنا معلم في مدرسة.
Pronunciation: Anā muʿallim fī madrasah.
Translation: I am a teacher at a school.

Dialogue 2: Discussing Workplaces

Scenario: You are discussing where you and your friend work.

Arabic: أين تعمل؟
Pronunciation: Ayna taʿmal?
Translation: Where do you work?

Arabic: أعمل في مستشفى.
Pronunciation: Aʿmal fī mustashfā.
Translation: I work in a hospital.

Arabic: أنا أعمل في شركة كبيرة.
Pronunciation: Anā aʿmal fī sharikah kabīrah.
Translation: I work at a big company.

Dialogue 3: Talking About Colleagues and Roles

Scenario: You are talking about your colleagues and what they do.

Arabic: هل تعمل مع زملاء آخرين؟
Pronunciation: Hal taʿmal maʿ zumalāʾ ākharīn?
Translation: Do you work with other colleagues?

Arabic: نعم، أعمل مع مهندسين آخرين.
Pronunciation: Naʿam, aʿmal maʿ muhandisīn ākharīn.
Translation: Yes, I work with other engineers.

Arabic: من هو مديرك؟
Pronunciation: Man huwa mudīruka?
Translation: Who is your manager?

Arabic: مديرنا رجل طيب ويعمل بجد.
Pronunciation: Mudīrunā rajul ṭayyib wa yaʿmal bijidd.
Translation: Our manager is a kind man and works hard.

Arabic: ماذا يفعل زميلك؟
Pronunciation: Mādhā yafʿal zamīluk?
Translation: What does your colleague do?

Arabic: زميلي محاسب في نفس الشركة.
Pronunciation: Zamīlī muḥāsib fī nafs ash-sharikah.
Translation: My colleague is an accountant at the same company.

Exercise:

Translate the following sentences into Arabic

1. I am an engineer.
2. My brother works as a lawyer.
3. She is a nurse at a hospital.
4. What does your father do for a living?
5. My mother works in a school.
6. I work at a big company.
7. He is a driver.
8. She is a cook at a restaurant.
9. I have a friend who is a police officer.
10. My uncle is a teacher.
11. I work as a programmer.
12. Do you work with other people?
13. My cousin is a doctor.
14. Where do you work?
15. I work with a team of engineers.
16. Our manager is very experienced.
17. I am a worker at a construction site.
18. He works in a hospital as a doctor.
19. My sister is a lawyer.
20. Do you work at a company or a hospital?

Chapter 5
Daily Routines

Key Vocabulary:

Arabic	Pronunciation	Translation
صباحًا	Ṣabāḥan	In the morning
مساءً	Masā'an	In the evening
أستيقظ	Astayqiẓ	I wake up
أذهب	Adhhab	I go
أعود	Aʿūd	I return
أتناول	Atanāwal	I eat
أدرس	Adrūs	I study
أعمل	Aʿmal	I work
أنام	Anām	I sleep
أقرأ	Aqra'	I read
أغسل	Aghsil	I wash
أطبخ	Aṭbukh	I cook
أمارس الرياضة	Umāris ar-Riyāḍah	I exercise
أذهب إلى العمل	Adhhab ila al-ʿamal	I go to work
المدرسة	Al-madrasah	School
الجامعة	Al-jāmiʿah	University
أتناول الإفطار	Atanāwal al-ifṭār	I have breakfast
أتناول الغداء	Atanāwal al-ghadā’	I have lunch
أتناول العشاء	Atanāwal al-ʿashā’	I have dinner
أخرج	Akhruj	I go out
يوميًا	Yawmiyan	Daily

Dialogue 1: Morning Routine

Scenario: You are talking to a friend about your morning routine.

Arabic: ماذا تفعل صباحًا؟
Pronunciation: Mādhā taf'al ṣabāḥan?
Translation: What do you do in the morning?

Arabic: أستيقظ في الساعة السابعة وأتناول الإفطار.
Pronunciation: Astayqiẓ fī as-sā'ah as-sābi'ah wa atanāwal al-ifṭār.
Translation: I wake up at 7 o'clock and have breakfast.

Arabic: هل تذهب إلى العمل بعد الإفطار؟
Pronunciation: Hal tadhhab ila al-'amal ba'da al-ifṭār?
Translation: Do you go to work after breakfast?

Arabic: نعم، أذهب إلى العمل في الساعة الثامنة.
Pronunciation: Na'am, adhhab ila al-'amal fī as-sā'ah ath-thāminah.
Translation: Yes, I go to work at 8 o'clock.

Dialogue 2: Afternoon and Evening Routine:

Scenario: You are discussing what you do in the afternoon and evening with a colleague.

Arabic: ماذا تفعل بعد الظهر؟
Pronunciation: Mādhā taf'al ba'da aẓ-ẓuhr?
Translation: What do you do in the afternoon?

Arabic: أتناول الغداء وأعود إلى المنزل.
Pronunciation: Atanāwal al-ghadā’ wa aʿūd ila al-manzil.
Translation: I have lunch and return home.

Arabic: وماذا تفعل مساءً؟
Pronunciation: Wa mādhā tafʿal masā'an?
Translation: And what do you do in the evening?

Arabic: أقرأ كتابًا أو أشاهد التلفاز.
Pronunciation: Aqra' kitāban aw ushāhid at-tilfāz.
Translation: I read a book or watch TV.

Dialogue 3: Discussing Night-time Routine:
Scenario: You are talking about your routine at night.

Arabic: في أي وقت تذهب إلى النوم؟
Pronunciation: Fī ayyi waqt tadhhab ila an-nawm?
Translation: At what time do you go to sleep?

Arabic: أنام في الساعة العاشرة.
Pronunciation: Anām fī as-sāʿah al-ʿāshirah.
Translation: I sleep at 10 o'clock.

Arabic: هل تمارس الرياضة قبل النوم؟
Pronunciation: Hal tumāris ar-riyāḍah qabl an-nawm?
Translation: Do you exercise before sleeping?

Arabic: نعم، أمارس الرياضة مساءً قبل العشاء.

Pronunciation: Naʿam, umāris ar-riyāḍah masā'an qabl al-ʿashā'.

Translation: Yes, I exercise in the evening before dinner.

Exercise:

Translate the following sentences into Arabic

1. I wake up at 6 in the morning.
2. I go to work after breakfast.
3. In the afternoon, I study at the university.
4. I read a book in the evening.
5. I go to sleep at 9 o'clock.
6. What do you do in the morning?
7. I eat lunch at 2 o'clock.
8. I exercise every day.
9. I work in the evening.
10. I go to school in the morning.
11. I return home after work.
12. I watch TV before dinner.
13. I have breakfast with my family.
14. I study Arabic at night.
15. I cook dinner every day.
16. I go out with friends on the weekend.
17. I wash my clothes in the evening.
18. I have dinner at 7 o'clock.
19. What time do you go to bed?
20. I leave the house at 8 in the morning.

Chapter 6
Ordering at a Restaurant

Key Vocabulary:

Arabic	Pronunciation	Translation
مطعم	Maṭʿam	Restaurant
قائمة الطعام	Qā'imat aṭ-ṭaʿām	Menu
طعام	Ṭaʿām	Food
شراب	Sharāb	Drink
طبق	Ṭabaq	Dish
لحم	Laḥm	Meat
دجاج	Dajāj	Chicken
سمك	Samak	Fish
خضار	Khuḍār	Vegetables
سلطة	Salāṭah	Salad
أرز	Ruzz	Rice
خبز	Khubz	Bread
ماء	Mā'	Water
شاي	Shāy	Tea
قهوة	Qahwah	Coffee
حلوى	Ḥalwā	Dessert
حساب	Ḥisāb	Bill/Check
كم السعر؟	Kam as-siʿr?	How much is it?
لذيذ	Ladhīdh	Delicious
أنا جائع	Anā jāʾiʿ	I am hungry
الفاتورة	Al-fātūrah	The bill

Arabic	Pronunciation	Translation
أريد	Urīd	I want
بدون	Bidūn	Without
مع	Maʿ	With
قليلاً	Qalīlan	A little
هل لديك	Hal ladayka	Do you have?

Dialogue 1: Arriving at the Restaurant:

Scenario: You arrive at a restaurant and speak to the waiter.

Arabic: مرحبًا، أريد طاولة لشخصين.
Pronunciation: Marḥabān, urīd ṭāwilah li-shakhsayn.
Translation: Hello, I would like a table for two.

Arabic: تفضل، هنا قائمة الطعام.
Pronunciation: Tafaddal, hunā qā'imat aṭ-ṭaʿām.
Translation: Please, here is the menu.

Arabic: شكرًا، هل لديكم أطباق نباتية؟
Pronunciation: Shukran, hal ladaykum aṭbāq nabātiyah?
Translation: Thank you, do you have vegetarian dishes?

Arabic: نعم، لدينا سلطة وخضار.
Pronunciation: Naʿam, ladaynā salāṭah wa khuḍār.
Translation: Yes, we have salad and vegetables.

Dialogue 2: Ordering Food:

Scenario: You are ready to order your food.

Arabic: ماذا تفضل أن تأكل؟
Pronunciation: Mādhā tufaddil an taʾkul?
Translation: What would you like to eat?

Arabic: أريد دجاج مع أرز وسلطة.
Pronunciation: Urīd dajāj maʿ ruzz wa salāṭah.
Translation: I want chicken with rice and salad.

Arabic: وماذا عن الشراب؟
Pronunciation: Wa mādhā ʿan ash-sharāb?
Translation: And what about the drink?

Arabic: ماء وقهوة من فضلك.
Pronunciation: Mā' wa qahwah min faḍlik.
Translation: Water and coffee, please.

Arabic: هل تريد شيئًا آخر؟
Pronunciation: Hal turīd shay'an ākhar?
Translation: Would you like anything else?

Arabic: لا، هذا كل شيء. شكرًا.
Pronunciation: Lā, hādhā kullu shay'. Shukran.
Translation: No, that's all. Thank you.

Dialogue 3: Asking for the Bill:

Scenario: You have finished eating and want to ask for the bill.

Arabic: هل يمكنني الحصول على الفاتورة؟
Pronunciation: Hal yumkinunī al-ḥuṣūl ʿalā al-fātūrah?
Translation: Can I have the bill?

Arabic: نعم، الفاتورة هنا. كم السعر؟
Pronunciation: Naʿam, al-fātūrah hunā. Kam as-siʿr?
Translation: Yes, here is the bill. How much is it?

Arabic: السعر عشرون دولارًا.
Pronunciation: As-siʿr ʿishrūn dūlāran.
Translation: The price is twenty dollars.

Arabic: شكرًا، كان الطعام لذيذًا جدًا.
Pronunciation: Shukran, kāna aṭ-ṭaʿām ladhīdh jiddan.
Translation: Thank you, the food was very delicious.

Arabic: شكرًا لكم، نراكم قريبًا.
Pronunciation: Shukran lakum, narākum qarīban.
Translation: Thank you, see you soon.

Exercise:

Translate the following sentences into Arabic

1. I am hungry, I want to eat now.
2. Do you have a table for four people?
3. I want fish with rice, please.
4. How much is the salad?
5. I want the drink without sugar.
6. This dish is delicious.
7. Can I have water, please?
8. I eat bread with my meal.
9. I want coffee in the morning.
10. I don't want meat, I want vegetables.
11. Do you have dessert?
12. I would like a menu, please.
13. The bill, please.

14. I am ready to order.
15. What do you recommend?
16. Do you have any chicken dishes?
17. I want my food with a little salt.
18. Can I have tea?
19. How much is the total?
20. Do you have vegetarian options?

Chapter 7

Shopping and Prices

Key Vocabulary:

Arabic	Pronunciation	Translation
تسوق	Tasawwuq	Shopping
سعر	Siʿr	Price
كم	Kam	How much?
غالي	Ghālī	Expensive
رخيص	Rakhīṣ	Cheap
متجر	Matjar	Store
سوق	Sūq	Market
مال	Māl	Money
حقيبة	Ḥaqībah	Bag
ملابس	Malābis	Clothes
حذاء	Ḥidhā'	Shoes
مقاس	Maqās	Size
كبير	Kabīr	Large
صغير	Ṣaghīr	Small
لون	Lawn	Color
أسود	Aswad	Black
أبيض	Abyaḍ	White
أحمر	Aḥmar	Red
أخضر	Akhḍar	Green
أزرق	Azraq	Blue
هل لديك	Hal ladayka	Do you have?
أريد	Urīd	I want

Arabic	Pronunciation	Translation
ممكن	Mumkin	Possible
تخفيض	Takhfīḍ	Discount
أشتري	Ashtarī	I buy
سأدفع	Sa'adfaʿ	I will pay
بطاقة ائتمان	Biṭāqat iʾtimān	Credit card
نقدًا	Naqdān	Cash

Dialogue 1: Asking About Items in a Store:

Scenario: You are shopping in a clothing store.

Arabic: مرحبًا، هل لديكم ملابس رجالية؟

Pronunciation: Marḥabān, hal ladaykum malābis rijāliyah?

Translation: Hello, do you have men's clothes?

Arabic: نعم، هنا قسم الملابس الرجالية.

Pronunciation: Naʿam, hunā qism al-malābis ar-rijāliyah.

Translation: Yes, here is the men's clothing section.

Arabic: أريد قميصًا أسود، كم السعر؟

Pronunciation: Urīd qamīṣan aswad, kam as-siʿr?

Translation: I want a black shirt, how much is it?

Arabic: السعر خمسون دولارًا.

Pronunciation: As-siʿr khamsūn dūlāran.

Translation: The price is fifty dollars.

Arabic: هذا غالي، هل هناك تخفيض؟
Pronunciation: Hādhā ghālī, hal hunāka takhfīḍ?
Translation: This is expensive, is there a discount?

Arabic: نعم، هناك تخفيض عشرة بالمئة.
Pronunciation: Naʿam, hunāka takhfīḍ ʿasharah bil-miʾah.
Translation: Yes, there is a ten percent discount.

Dialogue 2: Buying Groceries at the Market:
Scenario: You are at a market buying fruits and vegetables.

Arabic: كم سعر التفاح؟
Pronunciation: Kam siʿr at-tuffāḥ?
Translation: How much is the apple?

Arabic: التفاح بثلاثة دولارات للكيلوغرام.
Pronunciation: At-tuffāḥ bithalāthah dūlārat lil-kīlūghrām.
Translation: The apple is three dollars per kilogram.

Arabic: أريد كيلوغرامًا واحدًا من التفاح.
Pronunciation: Urīd kīlūghrāman wāḥidan min at-tuffāḥ.
Translation: I want one kilogram of apples.

Arabic: هل تحتاج شيئًا آخر؟
Pronunciation: Hal taḥtāj shay'an ākhar?
Translation: Do you need anything else?

Arabic: نعم، أريد خضار وبطاطا.
Pronunciation: Naʿam, urīd khuḍār wa baṭāṭā.
Translation: Yes, I want vegetables and potatoes.

Arabic: البطاطا بدولارين للكيلوغرام.
Pronunciation: Al-baṭāṭā bidūlārayn lil-kīlūghrām.
Translation: Potatoes are two dollars per kilogram.

Dialogue 3: Paying for Items:
Scenario: You are ready to pay for your items at the checkout counter.

Arabic: سأدفع نقدًا، كم الإجمالي؟
Pronunciation: Sa'adfaʿ naqdan, kam al-ijmālī?
Translation: I will pay cash, what is the total?

Arabic: الإجمالي خمسة وسبعون دولارًا.
Pronunciation: Al-ijmālī khamsah wa sabʿūn dūlāran.
Translation: The total is seventy-five dollars.

Arabic: هل يمكن الدفع ببطاقة ائتمان؟
Pronunciation: Hal yumkin ad-dafʿ bi-biṭāqat iʾtimān?
Translation: Can I pay with a credit card?

Arabic: نعم، نقبل بطاقة الائتمان.
Pronunciation: Naʿam, naqbalu biṭāqat al-iʾtimān.
Translation: Yes, we accept credit cards.

Arabic: شكرًا، كان التسوق ممتعًا.
Pronunciation: Shukran, kāna at-tasawwuq mumtiʿan.
Translation: Thank you, shopping was fun.

Exercise:

Translate the following sentences into Arabic

1. How much is the shirt?
2. I want a small size, please.
3. This bag is expensive.
4. Can I get a discount?
5. I want to buy shoes.
6. How much is this in cash?
7. Do you have red clothes?
8. I will pay with a credit card.
9. I like green and blue colors.
10. This price is too high.
11. I want to buy vegetables.
12. Is this possible with a discount?
13. The market is busy today.
14. Do you have white shoes?
15. The total is thirty dollars.
16. I need to buy a gift.
17. I am looking for a black shirt.
18. This price is cheap.
19. I like shopping at the market.
20. I want to buy this, how much is it?

Chapter 8

Describing People and Personalities

Key Vocabulary:

Arabic	Pronunciation	Translation
طويل	Ṭawīl	Tall
قصير	Qaṣīr	Short
سمين	Samīn	Fat
نحيف	Naḥīf	Thin
جميل	Jamīl	Beautiful
وسيم	Wasīm	Handsome
شعر	Sha'r	Hair
عيون	'Uyūn	Eyes
بشرة	Basharah	Skin
لطيف	Laṭīf	Kind
ذكي	Dhakī	Smart
مرح	Marīḥ	Fun
جاد	Jād	Serious
هادئ	Hādi'	Calm
عصبي	'Aṣabī	Nervous
كريم	Karīm	Generous
بخيل	Bakhīl	Stingy
متعاون	Muta'āwin	Helpful
أنيق	Anīq	Elegant
قوي	Qawī	Strong
ضعيف	Ḍa'īf	Weak
سعيد	Sa'īd	Happy

Arabic	Pronunciation	Translation
حزين	Ḥazīn	Sad
صبور	Ṣabūr	Patient
سريع الغضب	Sarīʿ al-ghaḍab	Quick-tempered

Dialogue 1: Describing Physical Appearance:

Scenario: You are describing a friend's appearance to someone.

Arabic: صديقي طويل ولديه شعر أسود.
Pronunciation: Ṣadīqī ṭawīl wa ladayhi shaʿr aswad.
Translation: My friend is tall and has black hair.

Arabic: كيف تبدو صديقتك؟
Pronunciation: Kayfa tabdū ṣadīqatuk?
Translation: How does your friend look?

Arabic: هي جميلة ولديها عيون زرقاء.
Pronunciation: Hiya jamīlah wa ladayhā ʿuyūn zarqāʾ.
Translation: She is beautiful and has blue eyes.

Arabic: هو نحيف ولكنه قوي.
Pronunciation: Huwa naḥīf walākinahu qawī.
Translation: He is thin but strong.
Arabic: لديه بشرة سمراء وهو أنيق دائمًا.
Pronunciation: Ladayhi basharah samrāʾ wa huwa anīq dāʾiman.
Translation: He has brown skin and is always elegant.

Dialogue 2: Describing Personalities:

Scenario: You are talking about the personalities of your coworkers.

Arabic: زميلي في العمل شخص لطيف وهادئ.
Pronunciation: Zamīlī fī al-ʿamal shakhs laṭīf wa hādiʾ.
Translation: My coworker is a kind and calm person.

Arabic: ماذا عن زميلتك؟
Pronunciation: Mādhā ʿan zamīlatik?
Translation: What about your coworker?

Arabic: هي ذكية جدًا لكنها عصبية قليلاً.
Pronunciation: Hiya dhakīyah jiddan lākinahā ʿaṣabīyah qalīlan.
Translation: She is very smart but a little nervous.

Arabic: مديري كريم ومتعاون.
Pronunciation: Mudīrī karīm wa mutaʿāwin.
Translation: My manager is generous and helpful.

Arabic: أحب الأشخاص المرحين أكثر من الجادين.
Pronunciation: Uḥibbu al-ashkhāṣ al-marīḥīn akthar min al-jādīn.
Translation: I like fun people more than serious ones.

Dialogue 3: Complimenting and Expressing Feelings:

Scenario: You are complimenting someone and expressing your feelings about them.

Arabic: أنتِ تبدين جميلة اليوم!
Pronunciation: Anti tabdīn jamīlah al-yawm!
Translation: You look beautiful today!

Arabic: شكرًا، أنت لطيف جدًا.
Pronunciation: Shukran, anta laṭīf jiddan.
Translation: Thank you, you are very kind.

Arabic: أشعر بالسعادة معك.
Pronunciation: Ashʿur bi-saʿādah maʿak.
Translation: I feel happy with you.

Arabic: وأنت شخص صبور، أحب هذا فيك.
Pronunciation: Wa anta shakhs ṣabūr, uḥibbu hādhā fīk.
Translation: And you are patient, I love that about you.

Arabic: أنا أحيانًا سريع الغضب، آسف.
Pronunciation: Anā aḥyānan sarīʿ al-ghaḍab, āsif.
Translation: I am sometimes quick-tempered, sorry.

Exercise:

Translate the following sentences into Arabic

1. My sister is beautiful and kind.
2. He is tall but weak.
3. She has blue eyes and blonde hair.
4. My father is calm and serious.
5. I am a little nervous today.
6. You are generous and elegant.
7. He is strong and smart.
8. I like patient people.
9. She looks beautiful in red.
10. He is quick-tempered sometimes.
11. My friend is kind and helpful.
12. She is fun and always smiling.
13. He has a serious personality.
14. My mother is thin and kind.

15. You are very smart.
16. She is short and has green eyes.
17. My brother is strong but calm.
18. She is a little bit shy but kind.
19. I am happy with my friend.
20. He is generous and always smiling.

Chapter 9

Talking About Hobbies and Free Time

Key Vocabulary:

Arabic	Pronunciation	Translation
هواية	Hiwāyah	Hobby
وقت الفراغ	Waqt al-farāgh	Free time
القراءة	Al-qirā'ah	Reading
الكتابة	Al-kitābah	Writing
الرسم	Al-rasm	Drawing/Painting
الرياضة	Al-riyāḍah	Sports
كرة القدم	Kurat al-qadam	Football/Soccer
السباحة	Al-sibāḥah	Swimming
الطبخ	Al-ṭabkh	Cooking
السفر	Al-safar	Traveling
الموسيقى	Al-mūsīqā	Music
الغناء	Al-ghinā'	Singing
الرقص	Al-raqṣ	Dancing
التصوير	Al-taṣwīr	Photography
مشاهدة التلفاز	Mushāhadat al-tilfāz	Watching TV
ركوب الدراجات	Rukūb al-darājāt	Cycling
لعب	La'ib	Playing
الخروج مع الأصدقاء	Al-khurūj ma' al-aṣdiqā'	Going out with friends
الجري	Al-jary	Running
التسوق	Al-tasawwuq	Shopping

Dialogue 1: Discussing Hobbies:

Scenario: Two friends are talking about their hobbies.

Arabic: ما هي هوايتك المفضلة؟
Pronunciation: Mā hiya hiwāyatuk al-mufaḍḍalah?
Translation: What is your favourite hobby?

Arabic: أحب القراءة والكتابة في وقت الفراغ.
Pronunciation: Uḥibbu al-qirā'ah wa al-kitābah fī waqt al-farāgh.
Translation: I like reading and writing in my free time.

Arabic: وأنا أحب الرسم والسباحة، ماذا عنك؟
Pronunciation: Wa anā uḥibbu al-rasm wa al-sibāḥah, mādhā 'ank?
Translation: And I like drawing and swimming, what about you?

Arabic: أحب لعب كرة القدم والخروج مع الأصدقاء.
Pronunciation: Uḥibbu la'ib kurat al-qadam wa al-khurūj ma' al-aṣdiqā'.
Translation: I like playing football and going out with friends.

Arabic: هل تحب السفر؟
Pronunciation: Hal tuḥibbu al-safar?
Translation: Do you like traveling?

Arabic: نعم، السفر هو هوايتي المفضلة.
Pronunciation: Na'am, al-safar huwa hiwāyatī al-mufaḍḍalah.
Translation: Yes, traveling is my favourite hobby.

Dialogue 2: Free Time Activities:

Scenario: A conversation about how to spend free time during weekends.

Arabic: ماذا تفعل في وقت الفراغ في عطلة نهاية الأسبوع؟
Pronunciation: Mādhā taf'al fī waqt al-farāgh fī 'uṭlat nihāyat al-usbū'?
Translation: What do you do in your free time on weekends?

Arabic: أحب مشاهدة التلفاز والاستماع إلى الموسيقى.
Pronunciation: Uḥibbu mushāhadat al-tilfāz wa al-istimā' ilā al-mūsīqā.
Translation: I like watching TV and listening to music.

Arabic: أنا أيضًا أحب الموسيقى وأحيانًا أغني.
Pronunciation: Anā ayḍan uḥibbu al-mūsīqā wa aḥyānan ughannī.
Translation: I also love music and sometimes I sing.

Arabic: هل تمارس الرياضة؟
Pronunciation: Hal tumāris al-riyāḍah?
Translation: Do you play sports?

Arabic: نعم، ألعب كرة القدم وأركب الدراجة.
Pronunciation: Na'am, al'ab kurat al-qadam wa arkub al-darājah.
Translation: Yes, I play football and ride a bicycle.

Arabic: رائع! أنا أحب الجري في الحديقة.
Pronunciation: Rā'i'! Anā uḥibbu al-jary fī al-ḥadīqah.
Translation: Great! I love running in the park.

Dialogue 3: Expressing Interest and Preferences:
Scenario: Two friends are discussing their preferences in hobbies.

Arabic: هل تحب التصوير؟
Pronunciation: Hal tuḥibbu al-taṣwīr?
Translation: Do you like photography?

Arabic: نعم، أحب التقاط الصور أثناء السفر.
Pronunciation: Naʿam, uḥibbu iltqāṭ al-ṣuwar athnāʾ al-safar.
Translation: Yes, I like taking photos while traveling.

Arabic: وأنا أحب الطبخ، أعد الأطباق الجديدة في وقت الفراغ.
Pronunciation: Wa anā uḥibbu al-ṭabkh, uʿidd al-aṭbāq al-jadīdah fī waqt al-farāgh.
Translation: And I love cooking, I make new dishes in my free time.

Arabic: رائع، يجب أن تجرب أطباقي يومًا ما!
Pronunciation: Rāʾiʿ, yajibu an tujarrib aṭbāqī yawman mā!
Translation: Great, you should try my dishes someday!

Arabic: بالتأكيد، وأنت يجب أن تصورني أثناء اللعب.
Pronunciation: Bil-taʾkīd, wa anta yajibu an tuṣawwirnī athnāʾ al-laʿib.
Translation: Sure, and you should take my photos while playing.

Exercise:

Translate the following sentences into Arabic

1. I love reading books in my free time.
2. He likes drawing and painting.
3. She loves to cook new dishes.
4. We go swimming on weekends.
5. They enjoy playing football.
6. I watch TV every evening.
7. She listens to music every day.
8. He likes cycling with his friends.
9. My favourite hobby is traveling.
10. I take photos of nature.
11. She enjoys dancing.
12. He goes running in the morning.
13. I play football with my brother.
14. We go shopping on Fridays.
15. He likes to sing in his free time.
16. I enjoy writing stories.
17. She is good at photography.
18. We love going out with friends.
19. He likes sports and running.
20. She spends her free time drawing.

Chapter 10

Asking for Directions

Key Vocabulary:

Arabic	Pronunciation	Translation
الاتجاهات	Al-ittijāhāt	Directions
شارع	Shāriʿ	Street
طريق	Ṭarīq	Road
قريب	Qarīb	Near
بعيد	Baʿīd	Far
أمام	Amām	In front of
خلف	Khalf	Behind
بجانب	Bijānib	Next to
يسار	Yasār	Left
يمين	Yamīn	Right
مباشرةً	Mubāsharatan	Straight
تقاطع	Taqāṭuʿ	Intersection
إشارة المرور	Ishārat al-murūr	Traffic light
محطة	Maḥaṭṭah	Station
ساحة	Sāḥah	Square
قريب من	Qarīb min	Close to
بعيد عن	Baʿīd ʿan	Far from
مركز المدينة	Markaz al-madīnah	City center
مكان	Makān	Place
أين	Ayn	Where

Dialogue 1: Asking for Directions to a Location:
Scenario: A person asks for directions to the nearest restaurant.

Arabic: عفواً، أين يوجد أقرب مطعم؟
Pronunciation: ʿAfwan, ayna yūjad aqrab maṭʿam?
Translation: Excuse me, where is the nearest restaurant?

Arabic: المطعم قريب من هنا، سر مباشرةً ثم اتجه يسارًا.
Pronunciation: Al-maṭʿam qarīb min hunā, sir mubāsharatan thumma ittajih yasāran.
Translation: The restaurant is near here, go straight, then turn left.

Arabic: هل المطعم خلف المحطة؟
Pronunciation: Hal al-maṭʿam khalf al-maḥaṭṭah?
Translation: Is the restaurant behind the station?

Arabic: لا، هو أمام محطة القطار بجانب البنك.
Pronunciation: Lā, huwa amām maḥaṭṭat al-qiṭār bijānib al-bank.
Translation: No, it's in front of the train station next to the bank.

Dialogue 2: Getting Directions to a Hotel:
Scenario: A tourist is asking how to get to a hotel.

Arabic: مرحبًا، كيف أصل إلى فندق السلام؟
Pronunciation: Marḥabān, kayfa aṣil ilā funduq al-salām?
Translation: Hello, how do I get to Al-Salam Hotel?

Arabic: اتجه يمينًا عند إشارة المرور، الفندق على يسارك.
Pronunciation: Ittajih yamīnan ʿinda ishārat al-murūr, al-funduq ʿalā yasārak.
Translation: Turn right at the traffic light, the hotel will be on your left.

Arabic: هل هو بعيد عن هنا؟
Pronunciation: Hal huwa baʿīd ʿan hunā?
Translation: Is it far from here?

Arabic: لا، ليس بعيدًا، يمكنك الوصول في خمس دقائق.
Pronunciation: Lā, laysa baʿīdan, yumkinuka al-wuṣūl fī khams daqāʾiq.
Translation: No, it's not far; you can get there in five minutes.

Dialogue 3: Navigating Through the City Center:
Scenario: A person is asking for directions to the city center.

Arabic: أين مركز المدينة من هنا؟
Pronunciation: Ayna markaz al-madīnah min hunā?
Translation: Where is the city center from here?

Arabic: سر مباشرةً ثم اتجه يمينًا عند التقاطع الأول.
Pronunciation: Sir mubāsharatan thumma ittajih yamīnan ʿinda al-taqāṭuʿ al-awwal.
Translation: Go straight, then turn right at the first intersection.

Arabic: وبعد ذلك؟
Pronunciation: Wa baʿda dhālik?
Translation: And after that?

Arabic: ستجد الساحة الكبيرة، مركز المدينة قريب منها.
Pronunciation: Satajidu al-sāḥah al-kabīrah, markaz al-madīnah qarīb minhā.
Translation: You will find the big square; the city center is nearby.

Arabic: شكرًا جزيلاً على المساعدة.
Pronunciation: Shukran jazīlan ʿalā al-musāʿadah.
Translation: Thank you very much for your help.

Exercise:

Translate the following sentences into Arabic

1. Where is the nearest market?
2. Go straight and turn left.
3. The station is far from here.
4. The bank is next to the post office.
5. Is the park behind the school?
6. The hotel is on the right.
7. Where is the main road?
8. Turn left at the intersection.
9. The bus station is near the square.
10. Go straight; the museum is on your left.
11. Is it close to the city center?
12. The hospital is far, about ten minutes by car.
13. Go straight, then turn right at the traffic light.
14. The library is behind the big building.
15. The supermarket is next to the pharmacy.
16. Can you tell me where the nearest bank is?
17. The restaurant is in front of the train station.
18. The mosque is on the left side of the street.
19. Is the café near the park?
20. The shopping mall is straight ahead, next to the hotel.

Chapter 11

Travel and Airports

Key Vocabulary:

Arabic	Pronunciation	Translation
المطار	Al-maṭār	Airport
الطائرة	Al-ṭāʾirah	Airplane
الرحلة	Al-riḥlah	Flight
جواز السفر	Jawāz al-safar	Passport
بطاقة الصعود	Biṭāqat al-ṣuʿūd	Boarding pass
أمتعة	Amtiʿah	Luggage
حقيبة	Ḥaqībah	Bag
الوزن	Al-wazn	Weight
بوابة	Bawwābah	Gate
الصعود	Al-ṣuʿūd	Boarding
الوصول	Al-wuṣūl	Arrival
المغادرة	Al-mughādarah	Departure
الجمارك	Al-jamārik	Customs
تأشيرة	Taʾshīrah	Visa
حزام الأمان	Ḥizām al-amān	Seatbelt
رحلة دولية	Riḥlah dawliyah	International flight
رحلة داخلية	Riḥlah dākhiliyah	Domestic flight
تأكيد الحجز	Taʾkīd al-ḥajz	Booking confirmation
تأخير	Taʾkhīr	Delay
مكتب الاستعلامات	Maktab al-istiʿlāmāt	Information desk

Dialogue 1: Checking In at the Airport:
Scenario: A traveler is checking in at the airport.

Arabic: صباح الخير، أود تأكيد حجز الرحلة إلى دبي.
Pronunciation: Ṣabāḥ al-khayr, awadd taʾkīd ḥajz al-riḥlah ilā Dubayy.
Translation: Good morning, I would like to confirm my flight booking to Dubai.

Arabic: أهلاً بك، هل يمكنني رؤية جواز السفر وبطاقة الحجز؟
Pronunciation: Ahlan bik, hal yumkinunī ruʾyat jawāz al-safar wa biṭāqat al-ḥajz?
Translation: Welcome, can I see your passport and booking ticket?

Arabic: تفضل، وهذه حقيبة اليد والأمتعة.
Pronunciation: Tafaddal, wa hādhihi ḥaqībat al-yad wa al-amtiʿah.
Translation: Here you go, and this is the handbag and luggage.

Arabic: الوزن جيد، وهذه بطاقة الصعود وبوابة رقم 5.
Pronunciation: Al-wazn jayid, wa hādhihi biṭāqat al-ṣuʿūd wa bawwābah raqam khamsah.
Translation: The weight is good, and here is your boarding pass. Gate No 5.

Arabic: شكرًا جزيلاً، متى يبدأ الصعود إلى الطائرة؟
Pronunciation: Shukran jazīlan, matā yabdaʾ al-ṣuʿūd ilā al-ṭāʾirah?
Translation: Thank you very much. When does boarding start?

Arabic: في الساعة التاسعة و النصف.
Pronunciation: Fī al-sāʿah al-tāsiʿah wa al-niṣf.
Translation: At 9:30.

Dialogue 2: Passing Through Security and Customs:
Scenario: A traveler passes through security and customs.

Arabic: هل لديك أي أشياء سائلة في الحقيبة؟
Pronunciation: Hal ladayka ayy ashyāʾ sāʾilah fī al-ḥaqībah?
Translation: Do you have any liquids in your bag?

Arabic: لا، فقط ملابس وجهاز الكمبيوتر المحمول.
Pronunciation: Lā, faqaṭ malābis wa jihāz al-kumbiyūtar al-maḥmūl.
Translation: No, just clothes and a laptop.

Arabic: يمكنك العبور، تفضل.
Pronunciation: Yumkinuka al-ʿubūr, tafaddal.
Translation: You can pass, go ahead.

Arabic: أين مكتب الجمارك؟
Pronunciation: Ayna maktab al-jamārik?
Translation: Where is the customs office?

Arabic: المكتب بجانب بوابة الخروج.
Pronunciation: Al-maktab bijānib bawwābat al-khurūj.
Translation: The office is next to the exit gate.

Dialogue 3: Asking for Assistance at the Airport:

Scenario: A traveler asks for help at the information desk.

Arabic: مرحبًا، أين يمكنني إيجاد مكتب الاستعلامات؟
Pronunciation: Marḥabān, ayna yumkinunī ījād maktab al-istiʿlāmāt?
Translation: Hello, where can I find the information desk?

Arabic: المكتب أمام بوابة رقم 10.
Pronunciation: Al-maktab amām bawwābah raqam ʿashrah.
Translation: The desk is in front of gate number 10.

Arabic: عندي مشكلة مع تأكيد الحجز، هل يمكنني المساعدة؟
Pronunciation: ʿIndī mushkilah maʿ taʾkīd al-ḥajz, hal yumkinunī al-musāʿadah?
Translation: I have an issue with booking confirmation. Can I get some help?

Arabic: بالطبع، أحتاج رؤية التأشيرة وبطاقة الرحلة.
Pronunciation: Bi-lṭabʿ, aḥtāj ruʾyat al-taʾshīrah wa biṭāqat al-riḥlah.
Translation: Of course, I need to see your visa and flight ticket.

Arabic: تأخرت الرحلة بسبب تأخير الطائرة.
Pronunciation: Taʾakhkharat al-riḥlah bisabab taʾkhīr al-ṭāʾirah.
Translation: The flight is delayed due to a delay in the airplane.

Exercise:

Translate the following sentences into Arabic

1. Where is the departure gate?
2. I need to check my luggage.
3. The flight is delayed by one hour.
4. The customs office is on the right.
5. Show your passport and boarding pass.
6. The airport is very busy today.
7. Where is the check-in counter?
8. My bag is too heavy; can I remove some items?
9. I am traveling on an international flight.
10. Where can I find the information desk?
11. The arrival hall is on the second floor.
12. Is the visa required for this flight?
13. I need to confirm my booking.
14. The plane will board at gate 7.
15. How many bags can I carry?
16. The flight is at 9 in the morning.
17. Where is the security checkpoint?
18. I need help finding my boarding gate.
19. Is there a delay in the departure?
20. Can I change my seat at the counter?

Chapter 12
Health and Visiting a Doctor

Key Vocabulary:

Arabic	Pronunciation	Translation
الطبيب	Al-ṭabīb	The doctor
المستشفى	Al-mustashfā	Hospital
العيادة	Al-ʿiyādah	Clinic
مريض	Marīḍ	Sick/Patient
ألم	Alam	Pain
صداع	Ṣudāʿ	Headache
حمى	Ḥummā	Fever
سعال	Suʿāl	Cough
دواء	Dawāʾ	Medicine
وصفة طبية	Waṣfah ṭibbiyah	Prescription
ضغط الدم	Ḍaghṭ al-dam	Blood pressure
فحص	Faḥṣ	Examination
موعد	Mawʿid	Appointment
الطوارئ	Al-ṭawāriʾ	Emergency
حرارة	Ḥarārah	Temperature
ألم في البطن	Alam fī al-baṭn	Stomach ache
دوخة	Dawkha	Dizziness
إسهال	Is'hāl	Diarrhea
التهاب	Iltihāb	Inflammation
حقنة	Ḥuqnah	Injection

Dialogue 1: Making an Appointment with a Doctor:

Scenario: A patient is calling to make an appointment with a doctor.

Arabic: مرحبًا، أود حجز موعد مع الطبيب.
Pronunciation: Marḥabān, awadd ḥajz maw'id ma'a al-ṭabīb.
Translation: Hello, I would like to book an appointment with the doctor.

Arabic: بالتأكيد، متى تود زيارة العيادة؟
Pronunciation: Bi-al-ta'kīd, matā tawadd ziyārat al-'iyādah?
Translation: Certainly, when would you like to visit the clinic?

Arabic: أريد الموعد اليوم، أشعر بآلام في البطن وصداع شديد.
Pronunciation: Urīd al-maw'id al-yawm, ashur bi-ālām fī al-baṭn wa ṣudā' shadīd.
Translation: I want the appointment today. I have stomach pain and a severe headache.

Arabic: لدينا موعد في الساعة الثالثة، هل يناسبك؟
Pronunciation: Ladaynā maw'id fī al-sā'ah al-thālithah, hal yunāsibuk?
Translation: We have an appointment at three o'clock. Does that work for you?

Arabic: نعم، هذا مناسب. شكرًا جزيلاً.
Pronunciation: Na'am, hādhā munāsib. Shukran jazīlan.
Translation: Yes, that works. Thank you very much.

Dialogue 2: Describing Symptoms to the Doctor:
Scenario: A patient describes their symptoms during a doctor's visit.

Arabic: مرحبًا دكتور، أشعر بألم في البطن وسعال مستمر.
Pronunciation: Marḥabān duktūr, ashur bi-ālam fī al-baṭn wa suʿāl mustamir.
Translation: Hello doctor, I feel pain in my stomach and have a persistent cough.

Arabic: منذ متى تشعر بهذه الأعراض؟
Pronunciation: Munthu matā tashʿur bihādhihi al-aʿrāḍ?
Translation: How long have you been experiencing these symptoms?

Arabic: منذ يومين، والحرارة مرتفعة أيضًا.
Pronunciation: Munthu yawmayn, wa al-ḥarārah murtafiʿah ayḍan.
Translation: For two days, and I also have a high temperature.

Arabic: سأقوم بفحص ضغط الدم والحرارة. من فضلك اجلس هنا.
Pronunciation: Saʾaqūm bi-faḥṣ ḍaghṭ al-dam wa al-ḥarārah. Min faḍlik iʿjlis hunā.
Translation: I will check your blood pressure and temperature. Please sit here.

Arabic: هل تحتاج إلى أدوية أو وصفة طبية؟
Pronunciation: Hal taḥtāj ilā adwiyah aw waṣfah ṭibbiyah?
Translation: Do you need any medication or a prescription?

Arabic: نعم، أرجو وصفة للدواء والسعال.
Pronunciation: Naʿam, arjū waṣfah li al-dawāʾ wa al-suʿāl.
Translation: Yes, I need a prescription for medicine and the cough.

Dialogue 3: At the Pharmacy:
Scenario: A patient is collecting medicine at the pharmacy.

Arabic: مرحبًا، أود استلام دوائي وفقًا لوصفة الطبيب.
Pronunciation: Marḥabān, awadd istalām dawāʾī wafqan li-waṣfah al-ṭabīb.
Translation: Hello, I would like to collect my medicine according to the doctor's prescription.

Arabic: بالطبع، هل لديك بطاقة الوصفة الطبية؟
Pronunciation: Bi-lṭabʿ, hal ladayka biṭāqat al-waṣfah al-ṭibbiyah?
Translation: Of course, do you have the prescription card?

Arabic: نعم، هذه هي الوصفة.
Pronunciation: Naʿam, hādhihi hiya al-waṣfah.
Translation: Yes, here is the prescription.

Arabic: هذه الأدوية يجب أن تأخذ مرتين في اليوم.
Pronunciation: Hādhihi al-adwiyah yajibu an taʾkhudh marratayn fī al-yawm.
Translation: These medicines should be taken twice a day.

Arabic: هل هناك أي تعليمات خاصة؟
Pronunciation: Hal hunāka ayy taʿlīmāt khāṣṣah?
Translation: Are there any special instructions?

Arabic: نعم، يجب تناول الدواء بعد الأكل.
Pronunciation: Naʿam, yajibu tanāwul al-dawāʾ baʿd al-akl.
Translation: Yes, the medicine should be taken after meals.

Exercise:

Translate the following sentences into Arabic

1. I have a headache and a fever.
2. Can I book an appointment with the doctor today?
3. The doctor said I need to rest.
4. I need to take the medicine three times a day.
5. Where is the emergency room in the hospital?
6. I feel dizzy and tired.
7. My child has a high fever and a cough.
8. The doctor is examining the patient now.
9. What is your blood pressure reading?
10. I have an appointment at the clinic at 10 o'clock.
11. I need medicine for a stomach ache.
12. How long have you been feeling this pain?
13. I will go to the hospital if my condition worsens.
14. Is there any pharmacy nearby?
15. I need an injection for the pain.
16. The doctor gave me a prescription for antibiotics.
17. I am feeling better after taking the medicine.
18. The nurse will check your temperature.
19. Do you have any allergies to medicine?
20. I have a pain in my chest; I need to see a doctor urgently.

Chapter 13

Weather and Seasons

Key Vocabulary:

Arabic	Pronunciation	Translation
الطقس	Al-ṭaqs	The weather
الجو	Al-jaww	The atmosphere
درجة الحرارة	Darajat al-ḥarārah	Temperature
الصيف	Al-ṣayf	Summer
الشتاء	Al-shitāʾ	Winter
الربيع	Al-rabīʿ	Spring
الخريف	Al-kharīf	Autumn/Fall
مشمس	Mushmis	Sunny
غائم	Ghāʾim	Cloudy
ممطر	Mumṭir	Rainy
ثلج	Thalj	Snow
ريح	Rīḥ	Wind
دافئ	Dāfiʾ	Warm
بارد	Bārid	Cold
عاصف	ʿĀṣif	Stormy
رطب	Raṭib	Humid
جاف	Jāf	Dry
جميل	Jamīl	Beautiful
سماء	Samāʾ	Sky
غروب	Ghurūb	Sunset

Dialogue 1: Talking About Today's Weather:

Scenario: Two friends are discussing the weather outside.

Arabic: كيف الطقس اليوم؟
Pronunciation: Kayfa al-ṭaqs al-yawm?
Translation: How is the weather today?

Arabic: الجو مشمس ودافئ، إنه يوم جميل!
Pronunciation: Al-jaww mushmis wa dāfiʾ, innahu yawm jamīl!
Translation: It's sunny and warm, it's a beautiful day!

Arabic: نعم، درجة الحرارة ثلاثون درجة.
Pronunciation: Naʿam, darajat al-ḥarārah thalāthūn darajah.
Translation: Yes, the temperature is thirty degrees.

Arabic: هل ستمطر في المساء؟
Pronunciation: Hal satumṭir fī al-masāʾ?
Translation: Will it rain in the evening?

Arabic: لا أعتقد، السماء صافية الآن.
Pronunciation: Lā aʿtaqid, al-samāʾ ṣāfiyah al-ān.
Translation: I don't think so, the sky is clear now.

Dialogue 2: Discussing the Seasons:

Scenario: A student asks their teacher about the different seasons in Arabic-speaking countries.

Arabic: ما هو الفصل المفضل لديك؟
Pronunciation: Mā huwa al-faṣl al-mufaḍḍal ladayk?
Translation: What is your favorite season?

Arabic: أحب الربيع، لأنه يكون لطيفًا ومزهرًا.
Pronunciation: Uḥibb al-rabīʿ, li-annahu yakūn laṭīfan wa muzharan.
Translation: I love spring because it's mild and blooming.

Arabic: وأنا أفضل الصيف، أحب الأيام الطويلة والشمس.
Pronunciation: Wa anā ufaḍḍil al-ṣayf, uḥibb al-ayyām al-ṭawīlah wa al-shams.
Translation: And I prefer summer; I love long days and the sun.

Arabic: هل الشتاء بارد في بلدك؟
Pronunciation: Hal al-shitāʾ bārid fī baladik?
Translation: Is winter cold in your country?

Arabic: نعم، يكون باردًا وممطرًا معظم الوقت.
Pronunciation: Naʿam, yakūn bāridan wa mumṭiran muʿẓam al-waqt.
Translation: Yes, it's cold and rainy most of the time.

Dialogue 3: Planning for a Trip Based on the Weather:

Scenario: A couple is planning a trip and discussing the weather forecast.

Arabic: هل سنذهب إلى الشاطئ هذا الأسبوع؟
Pronunciation: Hal sanadhhab ilā al-shāṭiʾ hādhā al-usbūʿ?
Translation: Are we going to the beach this week?

Arabic: دعني أتحقق من الطقس أولًا.
Pronunciation: Daʿnī ataḥaqqaq min al-ṭaqs awwalan.
Translation: Let me check the weather first.

Arabic: يقولون أن الطقس سيكون غائمًا وعاصفًا.
Pronunciation: Yaqūlūn anna al-ṭaqs sayakūn ghāʾiman wa ʿāṣifan.
Translation: They say the weather will be cloudy and stormy.

Arabic: إذًا، يجب أن نؤجل رحلتنا إلى الأسبوع القادم.
Pronunciation: Ithan, yajibu an nuʾajil riḥlatanā ilā al-usbūʿ al-qādim.
Translation: Then we should postpone our trip to next week.

Arabic: نعم، أتمنى أن يكون الجو مشمسًا ودافئًا.
Pronunciation: Naʿam, atamannā an yakūn al-jaww mushmisan wa dāfiʾan.
Translation: Yes, I hope the weather will be sunny and warm.

Exercise:

Translate the following sentences into Arabic

1. Today's weather is sunny and beautiful.
2. The temperature is cold in winter.
3. I love the spring season because of the flowers.
4. How is the weather in your city today?
5. It's raining, and the sky is cloudy.
6. Summer is hot and dry in my country.
7. I prefer autumn because it's cool and windy.
8. The weather forecast says it will snow tomorrow.
9. We need to wear warm clothes in winter.
10. I don't like humid weather; it's uncomfortable.
11. The sun sets at seven in the evening.
12. There is a storm coming this evening.
13. The weather is windy today; let's stay indoors.
14. It's a good day for a walk because it's cool and sunny.
15. Is it raining now, or is it still dry?
16. The sky is clear, and there are no clouds.
17. In autumn, the leaves fall from the trees.
18. What is the temperature today?
19. Summer is my favorite season because I love the sun.
20. I heard it will be a rainy day tomorrow.

Chapter 14

Time and Dates

Key Vocabulary:

Arabic	Pronunciation	Translation
وقت	Waqt	Time
ساعة	Sāʿah	Hour
دقيقة	Daqīqah	Minute
ثانية	Thāniyah	Second
اليوم	Al-yawm	Today
غدًا	Ghadan	Tomorrow
أمس	Ams	Yesterday
صباح	Ṣabāḥ	Morning
مساء	Masāʾ	Evening
الليل	Al-layl	Night
يوم	Yawm	Day
أسبوع	Usbūʿ	Week
شهر	Shahr	Month
سنة	Sanah	Year
تاريخ	Tārīkh	Date
الآن	Al-ān	Now
بعد	Baʿd	After
قبل	Qabl	Before
كم الساعة؟	Kam al-sāʿah?	What time is it?
متى	Matā	When
اليوم الاثنين	Al-yawm al-ithnayn	Today is Monday

Arabic	Pronunciation	Translation
الأسبوع القادم	Al-usbūʿ al-qādim	Next week
الشهر الماضي	Al-shahr al-māḍī	Last month
التاريخ	Al-tārīkh	The date

Dialogue 1: Asking for the Time:

Scenario: Two colleagues are meeting for a coffee break.

Arabic: كم الساعة الآن؟
Pronunciation: Kam al-sāʿah al-ān?
Translation: What time is it now?

Arabic: الساعة الثالثة والربع.
Pronunciation: Al-sāʿah al-thālithah wa al-rubʿ.
Translation: It's quarter past three.

Arabic: متى سنجتمع اليوم؟
Pronunciation: Matā sanajtamiʿ al-yawm?
Translation: When will we meet today?

Arabic: سنلتقي الساعة الخامسة مساءً.
Pronunciation: Sanaltaqī al-sāʿah al-khāmisah masāʾan.
Translation: We will meet at five in the evening.

Arabic: أتمنى ألا أتأخر.
Pronunciation: Atamannā allā ataʾkhar.
Translation: I hope I won't be late.

Dialogue 2: Discussing Dates and Schedules:

Scenario: A student is talking to a friend about scheduling a study session.

Arabic: متى سيكون الامتحان؟
Pronunciation: Matā sayakūn al-imtiḥān?
Translation: When will the exam be?

Arabic: الامتحان يوم الأربعاء القادم.
Pronunciation: Al-imtiḥān yawm al-arbiʿāʾ al-qādim.
Translation: The exam is next Wednesday.

Arabic: هل تستطيع الدراسة معي غدًا؟
Pronunciation: Hal tastaṭīʿ al-dirāsah maʿī ghadan?
Translation: Can you study with me tomorrow?

Arabic: نعم، سأكون متفرغًا في المساء.
Pronunciation: Naʿam, saʾakūn mutafarighan fī al-masāʾ.
Translation: Yes, I'll be free in the evening.

Arabic: جيد، لنبدأ الساعة السابعة.
Pronunciation: Jayyid, linabdaʾ al-sāʿah al-sābiʿah.
Translation: Good, let's start at seven.

Dialogue 3: Making Appointments:

Scenario: A person is calling a clinic to make an appointment with a doctor.

Arabic: أريد حجز موعد مع الطبيب.
Pronunciation: Urīd ḥajz mawʿid maʿ al-ṭabīb.
Translation: I want to book an appointment with the doctor.

Arabic: متى يناسبك الموعد؟
Pronunciation: Matā yunāsibuka al-mawʿid?
Translation: When is a good time for you?

Arabic: هل هناك موعد متاح غدًا في الصباح؟
Pronunciation: Hal hunāk mawʿid mutāḥ ghadan fī al-ṣabāḥ?
Translation: Is there an available appointment tomorrow morning?

Arabic: نعم، لدينا موعد في الساعة التاسعة.
Pronunciation: Naʿam, ladaynā mawʿid fī al-sāʿah al-tāsiʿah.
Translation: Yes, we have an appointment at nine o'clock.

Arabic: هذا ممتاز، سأكون هناك في الوقت المحدد.
Pronunciation: Hādhā mumtāz, saʾakūn hunāk fī al-waqt al-muḥaddad.
Translation: That’s perfect; I’ll be there on time.

Exercise:

Translate the following sentences into Arabic

1. What time is the meeting today?
2. The date today is the 15th of March.
3. I wake up at seven in the morning.
4. My birthday is next week.
5. We have a meeting at two o'clock in the afternoon.
6. What day is it today?
7. I am busy now; can we meet later?
8. The flight is on Friday at noon.
9. I am free on Sunday; let's meet then.
10. The class starts at ten and ends at eleven.
11. What is the time difference between our countries?
12. I will call you at eight in the evening.
13. Yesterday was a busy day at work.
14. Let's meet at the restaurant at six.
15. The weekend starts on Thursday evening.
16. How many hours are in a day?
17. We need to leave before the evening.
18. The event will take place next month.
19. What time will you arrive?
20. I will be ready in five minutes.

Chapter 15

Expressing Opinions and Preferences

Key Vocabulary:

Arabic	Pronunciation	Translation
أحب	Uḥibb	I like
لا أحب	Lā uḥibb	I don't like
أفضل	Ufaḍḍil	I prefer
أكره	Akrah	I hate
رأي	Raʾy	Opinion
في رأيي	Fī raʾyī	In my opinion
أعتقد أن	Aʿtaqid ʾanna	I think that
لا أعتقد	Lā aʿtaqid	I don't think
يعجبني	Yuʿjibunī	I like it
لا يعجبني	Lā yuʿjibunī	I don't like it
موافق	Muwāfiq	Agree
غير موافق	Ghayr muwāfiq	Disagree
أحب أن	Uḥibb ʾan	I would like to
أفضّل أن	Ufaḍḍil ʾan	I prefer to
ممتاز	Mumtāz	Excellent
جيد	Jayyid	Good
سيء	Sayyiʾ	Bad
أفضل	Afḍal	Better
أسوأ	Aswaʾ	Worse
جيد جدًا	Jayyid jiddan	Very good

Dialogue 1: Sharing Opinions About Food:

Scenario: Two friends are discussing their favourite types of food.

Arabic: ما نوع الطعام الذي تحبه؟
Pronunciation: Mā naw‘ al-ṭa‘ām alladhī tuḥibbuh?
Translation: What kind of food do you like?

Arabic: أحب الطعام الإيطالي، وخاصة البيتزا.
Pronunciation: Uḥibb al-ṭa‘ām al-īṭālī, wa khāṣṣatan al-bītzā.
Translation: I like Italian food, especially pizza.

Arabic: أما أنا، فأفضل الطعام العربي، مثل الكباب.
Pronunciation: Ammā anā, fa-uḍāfiḍ al-ṭa‘ām al-‘arabī, mithl al-kabāb.
Translation: As for me, I prefer Arabic food, like kebab.

Arabic: البيتزا جيدة، ولكن الكباب أفضل بكثير!
Pronunciation: Al-bītzā jayyidah, walākin al-kabāb afḍal bikaṯīr!
Translation: Pizza is good, but kebab is much better!

Arabic: أعتقد أن البيتزا أسوأ.
Pronunciation: A‘taqid ’anna al-bītzā aswa’.
Translation: I think pizza is worse.

Dialogue 2: Discussing Preferences in Movies:
Scenario: Two friends are talking about their movie preferences.

Arabic: ما نوع الأفلام التي تفضل مشاهدتها؟
Pronunciation: Mā nawʿ al-aflām allatī tufaḍḍil mushāhadatahā?
Translation: What kind of movies do you prefer to watch?

Arabic: أفضل الأفلام الكوميدية، فهي ممتعة.
Pronunciation: Ufaḍḍil al-aflām al-kūmīdiyyah, fahiya mumtiʿah.
Translation: I prefer comedy movies; they are enjoyable.

Arabic: في رأيي، الأفلام الرومانسية أفضل بكثير.
Pronunciation: Fī raʾyī, al-aflām al-rūmānsiyyah afḍal bikaṯīr.
Translation: In my opinion, romantic movies are much better.

Arabic: لا أوافق، أعتقد أن الأفلام الرومانسية مملة.
Pronunciation: Lā ʾuwāfiq, aʿtaqid ʾanna al-aflām al-rūmānsiyyah mumillah.
Translation: I disagree; I think romantic movies are boring.

Arabic: هذا رأيك، ولكن لكل شخص ذوقه.
Pronunciation: Hādhā raʾyuk, walākin likulli shakhṣ dhawqah.
Translation: That's your opinion, but everyone has their own taste.

Dialogue 3: Expressing Opinions About a New Product:
Scenario: Two colleagues are discussing a new product at work.

Arabic: ما رأيك في هذا المنتج الجديد؟
Pronunciation: Mā ra'yuk fī hādhā al-muntaj al-jadīd?
Translation: What do you think of this new product?

Arabic: في رأيي، التصميم ممتاز، لكن السعر مرتفع.
Pronunciation: Fī ra'yī, al-taṣmīm mumtāz, lākīn al-si'r murtafi'.
Translation: In my opinion, the design is excellent, but the price is high.

Arabic: نعم، أوافقك الرأي، السعر يجب أن يكون أقل.
Pronunciation: Na'am, 'uwāfiquka al-ra'y, al-si'r yajibu 'an yakūna aqall.
Translation: Yes, I agree with you, the price should be lower.

Arabic: إذا كان السعر أقل، فسأحب شرائه.
Pronunciation: 'idhā kān al-si'r aqall, fa-sa'uḥibb shirā'uh.
Translation: If the price were lower, I would like to buy it.

Arabic: أتفق معك، لكن يجب تحسين الجودة أيضًا.
Pronunciation: Atfiq ma'ak, lākīn yajibu taḥsīn al-jawdah aydan.
Translation: I agree with you, but the quality should also be improved.

Exercise:

Translate the following sentences into Arabic

1. I prefer tea over coffee.
2. In my opinion, this book is good.
3. I like movies, especially action movies.
4. I think this shirt is better than that one.
5. I don't like spicy food.
6. He prefers reading to watching TV.
7. This restaurant is good, but I think it's too expensive.
8. I agree; the service here is excellent.
9. I hate waiting in long lines.
10. What is your opinion about this movie?
11. I think the design is perfect.
12. Do you agree with my opinion?
13. I would like to try a different flavor.
14. I believe this brand is the best.
15. I like summer, but I prefer winter.
16. He doesn't like cold weather.
17. I think it's important to listen to everyone's opinion.
18. She prefers working alone.
19. I like the idea; it's very creative.
20. In my opinion, the quality could be better.

Chapter 16
Talking About Places and Directions

Key Vocabulary:

Arabic	Pronunciation	Translation
مكان	Makān	Place
شارع	Shāriʿ	Street
طريق	Ṭarīq	Road
قريب من	Qarīb min	Near
بعيد عن	Baʿīd ʿan	Far from
يمين	Yamīn	Right
يسار	Yasār	Left
أمام	Amām	In front of
خلف	Khalf	Behind
بجانب	Bijānib	Next to
مقابل	Muqābil	Opposite
وسط	Wasaṭ	Center
بالقرب من	Bilqurb min	Near
محطة	Maḥaṭṭah	Station
فندق	Funduq	Hotel
مستشفى	Mustashfā	Hospital
مطعم	Maṭʿam	Restaurant
سوق	Sūq	Market
مكتب	Maktab	Office
مكتبة	Maktabah	Library
ميدان	Mīdān	Square

Dialogue 1: Asking for Directions to a Hotel:

Scenario: A tourist is asking a local for directions to the nearest hotel.

Arabic: أين يقع أقرب فندق من هنا؟
Pronunciation: ʾayna yaqʿa aqrab funduq min hunā?
Translation: Where is the nearest hotel from here?

Arabic: الفندق قريب من هنا. اذهب إلى الأمام، ثم خذ يسارًا.
Pronunciation: Al-funduq qarīb min hunā. Idhhab ilā al-amām, thumma khudh yasāran.
Translation: The hotel is near here. Go straight, then take a left.

Arabic: هل هو بعيد عن محطة القطار؟
Pronunciation: Hal huwa baʿīd ʿan maḥaṭṭat al-qiṭār?
Translation: Is it far from the train station?

Arabic: لا، إنه قريب من محطة القطار.
Pronunciation: Lā, innahu qarīb min maḥaṭṭat al-qiṭār.
Translation: No, it's near the train station.

Dialogue 2: Asking About Locations in the City:

Scenario: A visitor is asking about various locations in the city.

Arabic: أين يمكنني أن أجد مكتبة قريبة؟
Pronunciation: ʾayna yumkinunī ʾan ʾajid maktabah qarībah?
Translation: Where can I find a nearby library?

Arabic: المكتبة في وسط المدينة، بجانب السوق.
Pronunciation: Al-maktabah fī wasaṭ al-madīnah, bijānib al-sūq.
Translation: The library is in the city center, next to the market.

Arabic: وأين يقع المستشفى؟
Pronunciation: Wa ʾayna yaqʿu al-mustashfā?
Translation: And where is the hospital located?

Arabic: المستشفى خلف الميدان، على الطريق الرئيسي.
Pronunciation: Al-mustashfā khalf al-mīdān, ʿalā al-ṭarīq al-raʾīsī.
Translation: The hospital is behind the square, on the main road.

Arabic: شكراً جزيلاً على المساعدة.
Pronunciation: Shukran jazīlan ʿalā al-musāʿadah.
Translation: Thank you very much for your help.

Dialogue 3: Giving Directions to a Restaurant:

Scenario: A local is giving directions to a tourist who is looking for a restaurant.

Arabic: هل يمكنك أن ترشدني إلى مطعم قريب؟
Pronunciation: Hal yumkinuka ʾan turshidanī ilā maṭʿam qarīb?
Translation: Can you guide me to a nearby restaurant?

Arabic: بالطبع، اذهب مباشرة إلى الأمام وستجد المطعم على اليمين.
Pronunciation: Bi-l-ṭabʿ, idhhab mubāsharatan ilā al-amām wa sa-tajid al-maṭʿam ʿalā al-yamīn.
Translation: Of course, go straight ahead, and you will find the restaurant on the right.

Arabic: هل هو بجانب الفندق؟
Pronunciation: Hal huwa bijānib al-funduq?
Translation: Is it next to the hotel?

Arabic: نعم، المطعم مقابل الفندق تمامًا.
Pronunciation: Naʿam, al-maṭʿam muqābil al-funduq tamāmān.
Translation: Yes, the restaurant is exactly opposite the hotel.

Arabic: فهمت، شكراً لك!
Pronunciation: Fahimt, shukran lak!
Translation: Got it, thank you!

Exercise:

Translate the following sentences into Arabic

1. The market is far from the office.
2. Go left, then turn right at the street.
3. The library is behind the school.
4. The hotel is in front of the restaurant.
5. Is the train station near the main road?
6. The office is in the center of the city.
7. The hospital is opposite the market.
8. The restaurant is next to the hotel.
9. Is there a pharmacy near here?
10. The road to the park is straight ahead.
11. The market is on the left side.
12. I need directions to the library.
13. The school is in the middle of the city.
14. The hotel is on the main street.
15. The bus station is near the library.
16. The coffee shop is next to the park.
17. Where is the main square located?
18. The bank is on the right side of the street.
19. I prefer to take the main road to the hotel.
20. Is there a parking lot near the market?

Chapter 17

Making and Cancelling Plans

Key Vocabulary:

Arabic	Pronunciation	Translation
خطة	Khuṭṭah	Plan
موعد	Maw'id	Appointment
اجتماع	Ijtimāʿ	Meeting
حجز	Ḥajz	Reservation
تأكيد	Ta'kīd	Confirmation
إلغاء	Iglā'	Cancellation
دعوة	Da'wah	Invitation
غدًا	Ghadan	Tomorrow
لاحقًا	Lāḥiqan	Later
مساءً	Masā'an	In the evening
صباحًا	Ṣabāḥan	In the morning
قريبًا	Qarīban	Soon
يوم	Yawm	Day
موعد جديد	Maw'id jadīd	New appointment
وقت	Waqt	Time
أتمنى	Atamanā	I hope
مشغول	Mashghūl	Busy
موعد الغداء	Maw'id al-ghadā'	Lunch appointment
تأجيل	Ta'jīl	Postponement
رفض	Rafd	Refusal

Dialogue 1: Making Plans with a Friend:
Scenario: Two friends are making plans to meet up for coffee.

Arabic: هل ترغب في الاجتماع غدًا؟
Pronunciation: Hal targhab fī al-ijtimāʿ ghadan?
Translation: Would you like to meet up tomorrow?

Arabic: نعم، أود ذلك. في أي وقت؟
Pronunciation: Naʿam, ʾawadd dhālika. Fī ʾay waqt?
Translation: Yes, I would like that. At what time?

Arabic: ما رأيك في الساعة الرابعة مساءً؟
Pronunciation: Mā raʾyuka fī al-sāʿah al-rābiʿah masāʾan?
Translation: How about 4 PM?

Arabic: الوقت مناسب جدًا. أين نلتقي؟
Pronunciation: Al-waqt munāsib jiddan. ʾAyna naltaqī?
Translation: The time is perfect. Where shall we meet?

Arabic: لنلتقي في المقهى بجانب المكتبة.
Pronunciation: Linaltaqī fī al-maqha bijānib al-maktabah.
Translation: Let's meet at the café next to the library.

Dialogue 2: Cancelling Plans and Rescheduling:
Scenario: One friend needs to cancel and reschedule a planned meeting.

Arabic: آسف، لن أستطيع الحضور غدًا. لدي اجتماع.
Pronunciation: ʾĀsif, lan ʾastaṭīʿ al-ḥuḍūr ghadan. Ladayya ijtimāʿ.
Translation: Sorry, I won't be able to attend tomorrow. I have a meeting.

Arabic: لا بأس، متى يمكنك أن تلتقي؟
Pronunciation: Lā baʾs, matā yumkinuka ʾan taltaqī?
Translation: No problem, when can you meet?

Arabic: هل يناسبك يوم الخميس مساءً؟
Pronunciation: Hal yunāsibuka yawm al-khamīs masāʾan?
Translation: Does Thursday evening suit you?

Arabic: نعم، يناسبني ذلك. سأراك في الموعد الجديد.
Pronunciation: Naʿam, yunāsibunī dhālika. Saʾarāk fī al-mawʿid al-jadīd.
Translation: Yes, that suits me. I'll see you at the new appointment.

Arabic: شكرًا لتفهمك.
Pronunciation: Shukran li-tafahhumik.
Translation: Thank you for your understanding.

Dialogue 3: Making a Reservation at a Restaurant:
Scenario: A person is calling to make a dinner reservation at a restaurant.

Arabic: مرحبًا، أود حجز طاولة لشخصين مساء الغد.
Pronunciation: Marḥaban, ʾawadd ḥajz ṭāwilah li-shakhsayn masāʾ al-ghad.
Translation: Hello, I would like to reserve a table for two tomorrow evening.

Arabic: بالتأكيد. هل تود تأكيد الحجز؟
Pronunciation: Bi-l-taʾkīd. Hal tawadd taʾkīd al-ḥajz?
Translation: Certainly. Would you like to confirm the reservation?

Arabic: نعم، أرجو أن يتم التأكيد.
Pronunciation: Naʿam, ʾarjū ʾan yatimm al-taʾkīd.
Translation: Yes, please confirm it.

Arabic: تم الحجز بنجاح. نراك غدًا.
Pronunciation: Tamm al-ḥajz bi-najāḥ. Narāk ghadan.
Translation: The reservation is successful. See you tomorrow.

Arabic: شكرًا لكم. إلى اللقاء.
Pronunciation: Shukran lakum. ʾIlā al-liqāʾ.
Translation: Thank you. Goodbye.

Exercise:

Translate the following sentences into Arabic

1. I have a meeting tomorrow.
2. Can we reschedule the appointment?
3. I want to confirm the reservation.
4. We have a plan to meet at 6 PM.
5. Sorry, I need to cancel the dinner.
6. Do you want to make a new plan?
7. I am busy on Friday.
8. Can you attend the meeting?
9. I hope to see you soon.
10. Let's meet later.
11. The reservation is for two people.
12. What time suits you?
13. Shall we meet in the morning?
14. I have an appointment at the office.
15. Can we make a plan for tomorrow?
16. I need to postpone the meeting.
17. The new time is perfect.
18. Thank you for changing the plan.
19. I am available on Saturday.
20. Let's confirm the plan for next week.

Chapter 18

Asking for Help and Assistance

Key Vocabulary:

Arabic	Pronunciation	Translation
مساعدة	Musāʿadah	Help
أحتاج	ʾAḥtāj	I need
هل يمكنك	Hal yumkinuka	Can you
بالطبع	Bi-l-ṭabʿ	Of course
من فضلك	Min faḍlik	Please
كيف أستطيع	Kayfa ʾastaṭīʿ	How can I
لا مشكلة	Lā mushkilah	No problem
هل تحتاج إلى	Hal taḥtāj ʾilā	Do you need
شكراً	Shukran	Thank you
مسرور بمساعدتك	Masrūr bi-musāʿadatik	Glad to help
أستطيع	ʾAstaṭīʿ	I can
أي خدمة	ʾAyy khidmah	Any service
مساعدة طبية	Musāʿadah ṭibbiyyah	Medical assistance
الإسعاف	Al-ʾisʿāf	Ambulance
الشرطة	Al-shurṭah	Police
الطوارئ	Al-ṭawāriʾ	Emergency
آسف	ʾĀsif	Sorry
عاجل	ʿĀjil	Urgent
مفقود	Mafqūd	Lost
خطر	Khaṭar	Danger

Dialogue 1: Asking for Help in Daily Situations:

Scenario: A person asks for help finding their way in a new place.

Arabic: هل يمكنك مساعدتي؟ أنا ضائع.
Pronunciation: Hal yumkinuka musāʿdatī? ʾAnā ḍāʾiʿ.
Translation: Can you help me? I am lost.

Arabic: بالطبع، كيف أستطيع مساعدتك؟
Pronunciation: Bi-l-ṭabʿ, kayfa ʾastaṭīʿ musāʿdatak?
Translation: Of course, how can I help you?

Arabic: أحتاج إلى الوصول إلى محطة القطار.
Pronunciation: ʾAḥtāj ʾilā al-wuṣūl ʾilā maḥaṭṭat al-qiṭār.
Translation: I need to get to the train station.

Arabic: لا مشكلة، إنها في الجهة اليمنى بعد الشارع الأول.
Pronunciation: Lā mushkilah, ʾinnahā fī al-jihat al-yumnā baʿd al-shāriʿ al-awwal.
Translation: No problem, it's on the right side after the first street.

Dialogue 2: Offering Help to a Friend:

Scenario: A person offers help to a friend who is struggling with carrying bags.

Arabic: هل تحتاج إلى مساعدة في حمل الحقائب؟
Pronunciation: Hal taḥtāj ʾilā musāʿadah fī ḥaml al-ḥaqāʾib?
Translation: Do you need help carrying the bags?

Arabic: نعم، شكراً لك. إنها ثقيلة جدًا.
Pronunciation: Naʿam, shukran lak. ʾInnahā thaqīlah jiddan.
Translation: Yes, thank you. They are very heavy.

Arabic: سأساعدك. لا تقلق.
Pronunciation: Saʾusāʿiduk. Lā taqlaq.
Translation: I will help you. Don't worry.

Arabic: أنت لطيف جدًا. شكرًا مرة أخرى.
Pronunciation: ʾAnta laṭīf jiddan. Shukran marrah ʾukhrā.
Translation: You are very kind. Thank you again.

Dialogue 3: Asking for Medical Assistance:
Scenario: A person asks for medical assistance for someone in need.

Arabic: هل يمكنك طلب الإسعاف؟ هناك شخص مريض.
Pronunciation: Hal yumkinuka ṭalab al-ʾisʿāf? Hunāk shakhs marīḍ.
Translation: Can you call the ambulance? There is a sick person.

Arabic: بالطبع، سأفعل ذلك فورًا.
Pronunciation: Bi-l-ṭabʿ, sa-ʾafʿal dhālika fawran.
Translation: Of course, I will do that immediately.

Arabic: شكرًا، الوضع عاجل.
Pronunciation: Shukran, al-waḍʿ ʿājil.
Translation: Thank you, the situation is urgent.

Arabic: الإسعاف في الطريق. هل هناك شيء آخر؟
Pronunciation: Al-ʾisʿāf fī al-ṭarīq. Hal hunāk shayʾ ʾākhar?
Translation: The ambulance is on the way. Is there anything else?

Arabic: لا، هذا يكفي. أنت رائع.
Pronunciation: Lā, hādhā yakfī. ʾAnt rāʾiʿ.
Translation: No, that's enough. You are amazing.

Exercise:

Translate the following sentences into Arabic

1. Can you help me with this?
2. I need urgent help.
3. How can I offer help?
4. The ambulance is coming soon.
5. Thank you for your assistance.
6. Do you need any help with this?
7. I am lost, can you guide me?
8. He needs medical help immediately.
9. Sorry, I cannot help right now.
10. Can you call the police, please?
11. I am glad to assist you.
12. No problem, I will handle it.
13. Is there any danger here?
14. I lost my way, can you help?
15. What kind of help do you need?
16. Please wait, I will get help.
17. I will call for help right away.
18. Are you in trouble? Do you need help?
19. Help is on the way, stay calm.
20. You are very kind, thank you.

Chapter 19

Social Media and Technology

Key Vocabulary:

Arabic	Pronunciation	Translation
إنترنت	ʾInternet	Internet
هاتف	Hātif	Phone
تطبيق	Taṭbīq	App
حساب	Ḥisāb	Account
شبكة اجتماعية	Shabakah ijtimāʿiyyah	Social network
تحميل	Taḥmīl	Download
نشر	Nashr	Post
صورة	Ṣūrah	Picture
رسالة	Risālah	Message
فيديو	Fīdīū	Video
تعليق	Taʿlīq	Comment
متابعة	Mutābaʿah	Follow
إلغاء المتابعة	Iglāʾ al-mutābaʿah	Unfollow
مشاركة	Mushārakah	Share
تسجيل الدخول	Tashjīl al-dukhūl	Login
كلمة المرور	Kalimat al-murūr	Password
بريد إلكتروني	Barīd ʾiliktirūnī	Email
فيديو مباشر	Fīdīū mubāshir	Live video
تقني	Taqanī	Tech-savvy
جهاز	Jihāz	Device

Dialogue 1: Discussing Social Media Usage
Scenario: Two friends talk about their social media habits.

Arabic: هل تستخدم الإنترنت كثيراً؟
Pronunciation: Hal tastaʿmil al-ʾinternet kathīran?
Translation: Do you use the internet a lot?

Arabic: نعم، أستخدمه يوميًا على هاتفي.
Pronunciation: Naʿam, ʾastaʿmiluhu yawmiyyan ʿalā hātifī.
Translation: Yes, I use it daily on my phone.

Arabic: ما هو تطبيقك المفضل؟
Pronunciation: Mā huwa taṭbīqak al-mufaḍḍal?
Translation: What is your favourite app?

Arabic: أحب تطبيق الإنستجرام لنشر الصور.
Pronunciation: ʾUḥibb taṭbīq al-ʾinstagrām li-nashr al-ṣuwar.
Translation: I like Instagram for posting pictures.

Arabic: وأنا أحب متابعة الفيديوهات على اليوتيوب.
Pronunciation: Wa-ʾanā ʾuḥibb mutābaʿat al-fīdīūhāt ʿalā al-yūtūb.
Translation: And I like watching videos on YouTube.

Dialogue 2: Troubleshooting Tech Issues
Scenario: A person asks for help with a technology problem.

Arabic: لا أستطيع تسجيل الدخول إلى حسابي.
Pronunciation: Lā ʾastaṭīʿ tashjīl al-dukhūl ʾilā ḥisābī.
Translation: I can't log into my account.

Arabic: هل نسيت كلمة المرور؟
Pronunciation: Hal nasīta kalimat al-murūr?
Translation: Did you forget your password?

Arabic: نعم، ولا أستطيع استعادتها.
Pronunciation: Naʿam, wa-lā ʾastaṭīʿ istiʿādatihā.
Translation: Yes, and I can't recover it.

Arabic: جرب استخدام البريد الإلكتروني لاستعادتها.
Pronunciation: Jarrib istiʿmāl al-barīd al-ʾiliktirūnī li-istiʿādatihā.
Translation: Try using the email to recover it.

Arabic: سأحاول الآن، شكرًا لك.
Pronunciation: Sa-ʾuḥāwil al-ʾān, shukran lak.
Translation: I will try now, thank you.

Dialogue 3: Talking About Technology Preferences
Scenario: A conversation about the impact of technology.

Arabic: ما رأيك في التكنولوجيا الحديثة؟
Pronunciation: Mā raʾyuk fī al-tiknulūjiyā al-ḥadīthah?
Translation: What do you think of modern technology?

Arabic: أعتقد أنها مفيدة جدًا في حياتنا اليومية.
Pronunciation: ʾAʿtaqid ʾannahā mufīdah jiddan fī ḥayātnā al-yawmiyyah.
Translation: I think it's very useful in our daily lives.

Arabic: نعم، ولكن في بعض الأحيان نصبح مدمنين عليها.
Pronunciation: Naʿam, walākin fī baʿḍ al-ʾaḥyān nuṣbiḥ mudminīn ʿalayhā.
Translation: Yes, but sometimes we become addicted to it.

Arabic: صحيح، يجب علينا التحكم في استخدامنا للتكنولوجيا.
Pronunciation: Ṣaḥīḥ, yajibu ʿalaynā al-taḥakkum fī istiʿmālinā lil-tiknulūjiyā.
Translation: True, we need to control our use of technology.

Arabic: أتفق معك. التكنولوجيا رائعة، لكن الاعتدال مهم.
Pronunciation: ʾAtafiq maʿak. Al-tiknulūjiyā rāʾiʿah, lākinn al-iʿtidāl muhimm.
Translation: I agree with you. Technology is great, but moderation is important.

Exercise:

Translate the following sentences into Arabic

1. I use my phone every day.
2. Can you help me log into my account?
3. I like to post pictures on social media.
4. What is your favourite app?
5. The internet is very useful.
6. I forgot my password, can you help?
7. I want to watch a video on YouTube.
8. Do you have an email account?
9. Please share the picture with me.
10. How can I download this app?
11. I enjoy watching live videos.

12. Social media is very popular.
13. Can you send me a message on my phone?
14. My device is not working, can you fix it?
15. I want to follow your account.
16. He likes to comment on posts.
17. I need to update my app.
18. She posted a video yesterday.
19. I prefer using my laptop for work.
20. Technology makes life easier.

Chapter 20

Describing Objects

Key Vocabulary:

Arabic	Pronunciation	Translation
كبير	Kabīr	Big
صغير	Ṣaghīr	Small
طويل	Ṭawīl	Long
قصير	Qaṣīr	Short
ثقيل	Thaqīl	Heavy
خفيف	Khafīf	Light
جميل	Jamīl	Beautiful
قبيح	Qabīḥ	Ugly
جديد	Jadīd	New
قديم	Qadīm	Old
مستدير	Mustadīr	Round
مربع	Murabbaʿ	Square
بلاستيك	Bilāstīk	Plastic
خشب	Khashab	Wood
معدن	Maʿdin	Metal
ناعم	Nāʿim	Soft
خشن	Khashin	Rough
أحمر	ʾAḥmar	Red
أزرق	ʾAzraq	Blue
أخضر	ʾAkhḍar	Green
أصفر	ʾAṣfar	Yellow

Dialogue 1: Describing a Bag
Scenario: Two friends are discussing a new bag.

Arabic: هل رأيت حقيبتي الجديدة؟
Pronunciation: Hal raʾayta ḥaqībatī al-jadīdah?
Translation: Have you seen my new bag?

Arabic: نعم، إنها كبيرة وجميلة.
Pronunciation: Naʿam, ʾinnahā kabīrah wa-jamīlah.
Translation: Yes, it's big and beautiful.

Arabic: هي أيضًا خفيفة وسهلة الحمل.
Pronunciation: Hiya ʾayḍan khafīfah wa-sahlah al-ḥaml.
Translation: It is also light and easy to carry.

Arabic: ما لونها؟
Pronunciation: Mā lawnuhā?
Translation: What color is it?

Arabic: لونها أزرق مع لمسات من الجلد البني.
Pronunciation: Lawnuhā ʾazraq maʿ lamasāt min al-jild al-bunnī.
Translation: Its color is blue with brown leather accents.

Dialogue 2: Discussing a Phone
Scenario: A person describes their new phone.

Arabic: اشتريت هاتفًا جديدًا أمس.
Pronunciation: Ishtaraytu hātifan jadīdan ʾams.
Translation: I bought a new phone yesterday.

Arabic: هل هو كبير؟
Pronunciation: Hal huwa kabīr?
Translation: Is it big?

Arabic: لا، هو صغير وخفيف.
Pronunciation: Lā, huwa ṣaghīr wa-khafīf.
Translation: No, it's small and light.

Arabic: هل هو مصنوع من البلاستيك؟
Pronunciation: Hal huwa maṣnūʿ min al-bilāstīk?
Translation: Is it made of plastic?

Arabic: لا، هو مصنوع من المعدن.
Pronunciation: Lā, huwa maṣnūʿ min al-maʿdin.
Translation: No, it's made of metal.

Arabic: يبدو جميلًا وحديثًا.
Pronunciation: Yabdū jamīlan wa-ḥadīthan.
Translation: It looks beautiful and modern.

Dialogue 3: Describing a Chair

Scenario: A person describes their favourite chair.

Arabic: هذا الكرسي قديم لكنه مريح جدًا.
Pronunciation: Hādhā al-kursī qadīm lākinnahu murīḥ jiddan.
Translation: This chair is old, but it's very comfortable.

Arabic: هل هو ثقيل؟
Pronunciation: Hal huwa thaqīl?
Translation: Is it heavy?

Arabic: نعم، إنه مصنوع من الخشب.
Pronunciation: Naʿam, ʾinnahū maṣnūʿ min al-khashab.
Translation: Yes, it's made of wood.

Arabic: يبدو مستديرًا ولونه بني داكن.
Pronunciation: Yabdū mustadīran wa-lawnuh bunnī dākin.
Translation: It looks round and its color is dark brown.

Arabic: أحبه لأنه ناعم ومريح.
Pronunciation: ʾUḥibbuhu li-ʾannah nāʿim wa-murīḥ.
Translation: I love it because it's soft and comfortable.

Exercise:

Translate the following sentences into Arabic

1. The table is round and made of wood.
2. This box is small and light.
3. I have a beautiful red dress.
4. The metal chair is heavy but strong.
5. My phone is new and made of plastic.
6. The old sofa is comfortable and soft.
7. The blue cup is big and heavy.
8. The car is long and red.
9. This pen is small and made of metal.
10. The bag is black and ugly.
11. The book is big and has a blue cover.
12. The box is light and square.
13. I like the yellow chair; it's comfortable.
14. The old phone is heavy and ugly.
15. This table is beautiful and round.
16. The watch is small and made of metal.

17. The picture is beautiful and colorful.
18. I bought a new blue bag yesterday.
19. This wooden chair is very comfortable.
20. The plastic cup is light and green.

Chapter 21

At the Hotel

Key Vocabulary:

Arabic	Pronunciation	Translation
فندق	Funduq	Hotel
غرفة	Ghurfah	Room
حجز	Ḥajz	Reservation
مفتاح	Miftāḥ	Key
خدمة	Khidmah	Service
استقبال	Istiqbāl	Reception
نظيف	Naẓīf	Clean
كبير	Kabīr	Big
صغير	Ṣaghīr	Small
مزدحم	Muzdahim	Crowded
مكيف	Mukayyaf	Air-conditioned
مطعم	Maṭʿam	Restaurant
بوفيه	Buffeh	Buffet
سعر	Siʿr	Price
أطلب	ʾAṭlub	I request
خدمة الغرف	Khidmat al-ghurf	Room service
مغسلة	Maghsalah	Laundry
اتصال	Ittiṣāl	Call
تأكيد	Tashkīd	Confirmation
خروج	Khurūj	Check-out

Dialogue 1: Checking In

Scenario: A guest is checking into the hotel.

Arabic: مرحبًا، أود تسجيل الدخول.
Pronunciation: Marḥabān, ʾawad tajjīl al-dukhūl.
Translation: Hello, I would like to check in.

Arabic: هل لديك حجز؟
Pronunciation: Hal ladayka ḥajz?
Translation: Do you have a reservation?

Arabic: نعم، حجزت غرفة مزدوجة.
Pronunciation: Naʿam, ḥajaztu ghurfah muzdawijah.
Translation: Yes, I reserved a double room.

Arabic: ما اسمك؟
Pronunciation: Mā ismuk?
Translation: What is your name?

Arabic: اسمي أحمد.
Pronunciation: Ismī Aḥmad.
Translation: My name is Ahmed.

Dialogue 2: Requesting Services

Scenario: A guest is asking for room service.

Arabic: هل يمكنني طلب خدمة الغرف؟
Pronunciation: Hal yumkinunī ʾaṭlubu khidmat al-ghurf?
Translation: Can I request room service?

Arabic: نعم، بالطبع. ماذا تريد؟
Pronunciation: Naʿam, bil-ṭabʿ. Mādhā turīd?
Translation: Yes, of course. What do you want?

Arabic: أريد طعامًا وعصيرًا.
Pronunciation: ʾUrīd ṭaʿāman wa-ʿaṣīran.
Translation: I want food and juice.

Arabic: حسنًا، سأحضره الآن.
Pronunciation: Ḥasanan, saʾuḥḍiruh al-ān.
Translation: Okay, I will bring it now.

Dialogue 3: Checking Out

Scenario: A guest is checking out of the hotel.

Arabic: أود الخروج الآن.
Pronunciation: ʾAwad al-khurūj al-ān.
Translation: I would like to check out now.

Arabic: هل لديك حساب لتسديده؟
Pronunciation: Hal ladayka ḥisāb li-tasdīdih?
Translation: Do you have a bill to settle?

Arabic: نعم، كم السعر؟
Pronunciation: Naʿam, kam al-siʿr?
Translation: Yes, what is the price?

Arabic: السعر هو مئة دولار.
Pronunciation: Al-siʿr huwa miʾah dūlār.
Translation: The price is one hundred dollars.

Arabic: شكرًا، سأدفع الآن.
Pronunciation: Shukran, saʾadfaʿ al-ān.
Translation: Thank you, I will pay now.

Exercise:

Translate the following sentences into Arabic

1. I have a reservation for a single room.
2. The hotel is clean and big.
3. Can I get a key for my room?
4. I need room service for dinner.
5. How much is the price per night?
6. Is there a restaurant in the hotel?
7. I would like to check out tomorrow.
8. The laundry service is very helpful.
9. The reception is on the first floor.
10. I want to make a call to my friend.
11. Is the air conditioning working?
12. The buffet has many delicious dishes.
13. My room is very comfortable and quiet.
14. Can I request a late check-out?
15. The hotel is crowded during the holidays.
16. I need a taxi to the airport.
17. The breakfast is included in the price.
18. Is there free Wi-Fi in the hotel?
19. I would like to change my room.
20. Thank you for your excellent service.

Chapter 22

Renting a House or Apartment

Key Vocabulary:

Arabic	Pronunciation	Translation
إيجار	ʾĪjār	Rent
شقة	Shaqqah	Apartment
منزل	Manzil	House
غرفة	Ghurfah	Room
حمام	Ḥammām	Bathroom
مطبخ	Maṭbakh	Kitchen
صالة	Ṣālah	Living room
عقد	ʿAqd	Contract
مالك	Mālik	Owner
مستأجر	Mustaʾjir	Tenant
توقيع	Tawqīʿ	Signature
مفروش	Mafrūsh	Furnished
غير مفروش	Ghayr mafrūsh	Unfurnished
وديعة	Wadīʿah	Deposit
كهرباء	Kahrabāʾ	Electricity
ماء	Māʾ	Water
إيجار شهري	ʾĪjār shahri	Monthly rent
السعر	Al-siʿr	Price
عقد الإيجار	ʿAqd al-ʾījār	Lease agreement
موقع	Mawqiʿ	Location
طابق	Ṭābiq	Floor

Dialogue 1: Inquiring About an Apartment
Scenario: A tenant is inquiring about renting an apartment.

Arabic: مرحبًا، هل لديك شقة للإيجار؟
Pronunciation: Marḥabān, hal ladayka shaqqah lil-ʾījār?
Translation: Hello, do you have an apartment for rent?

Arabic: نعم، لدينا شقة من ثلاث غرف.
Pronunciation: Naʿam, ladaynā shaqqah min thalāth ghuraf.
Translation: Yes, we have a three-room apartment.

Arabic: كم السعر الشهري؟
Pronunciation: Kam al-siʿr al-shahri?
Translation: What is the monthly rent?

Arabic: الإيجار الشهري هو ٥٠٠ دولار.
Pronunciation: Al-ʾījār al-shahri huwa khamsūn dūlār.
Translation: The monthly rent is $500.

Arabic: هل هي مفروشة؟
Pronunciation: Hal hiya mafrūshah?
Translation: Is it furnished?

Arabic: نعم، الشقة مفروشة بالكامل.
Pronunciation: Naʿam, al-shaqqah mafrūshah bi-l-kāmil.
Translation: Yes, the apartment is fully furnished.

Dialogue 2: Discussing the Lease Agreement

Scenario: The tenant and owner discuss the lease agreement.

Arabic: ما هي مدة عقد الإيجار؟

Pronunciation: Mā hiya muddah ʿaqd al-ʾījār?

Translation: What is the duration of the lease?

Arabic: مدة العقد سنة واحدة.

Pronunciation: Muddah al-ʿaqd sanah wāḥidah.

Translation: The contract duration is one year.

Arabic: هل يجب دفع وديعة؟

Pronunciation: Hal yajibu dafaʿ wadīʿah?

Translation: Is a deposit required?

Arabic: نعم، الوديعة هي إيجار شهر واحد.

Pronunciation: Naʿam, al-wadīʿah hiya ʾījār shahr wāḥid.

Translation: Yes, the deposit is one month's rent.

Arabic: هل يشمل الإيجار الماء والكهرباء؟

Pronunciation: Hal yashmal al-ʾījār al-māʾ wa-l-kahrabāʾ?

Translation: Does the rent include water and electricity?

Arabic: لا، الكهرباء والماء غير مشمولان.

Pronunciation: Lā, al-kahrabāʾ wa-al-māʾ ghayr mashmūlān.

Translation: No, electricity and water are not included.

Dialogue 3: Viewing the Apartment

Scenario: The tenant views the apartment with the owner.

Arabic: هل يمكنني رؤية الشقة الآن؟
Pronunciation: Hal yumkinunī ruʾyat al-shaqqah al-ān?
Translation: Can I see the apartment now?

Arabic: بالطبع، تفضل معي.
Pronunciation: Bil-ṭabʿ, tafḍal maʿī.
Translation: Of course, please come with me.

Arabic: الشقة جميلة جدًا وفيها صالة واسعة.
Pronunciation: Al-shaqqah jamīlah jiddan wa-fīhā ṣālah wāsiʿah.
Translation: The apartment is very beautiful and has a spacious living room.

Arabic: هل يوجد حمامان؟
Pronunciation: Hal yūjad ḥammāmān?
Translation: Are there two bathrooms?

Arabic: نعم، هناك حمامان ومطبخ كبير.
Pronunciation: Naʿam, hunāk ḥammāmān wa-maṭbakh kabīr.
Translation: Yes, there are two bathrooms and a large kitchen.

Arabic: في أي طابق تقع الشقة؟
Pronunciation: Fī ʾay ṭābiq taqaʿ al-shaqqah?
Translation: On which floor is the apartment located?

Arabic: الشقة في الطابق الثاني.
Pronunciation: Al-shaqqah fī al-ṭābiq al-thānī.
Translation: The apartment is on the second floor.

Arabic: أحببت الموقع والمساحة.
Pronunciation: ʾAḥbabtu al-mawqiʿ wa-al-masāḥah.
Translation: I liked the location and the space.

Exercise:

Translate the following sentences into Arabic

1. The apartment is big and has two rooms.
2. How much is the rent for the house?
3. The contract is for one year.
4. I would like to rent a furnished apartment.
5. The kitchen is small but clean.
6. Is the deposit refundable?
7. The apartment is on the third floor.
8. I need a house with a large living room.
9. Does the rent include water and electricity?
10. I am looking for an unfurnished apartment.
11. The bathroom is modern and spacious.
12. Can I sign the lease agreement today?
13. The owner is very kind and helpful.
14. I want to view the house before renting.
15. The price is high; can we negotiate?
16. Is there a laundry room in the apartment?
17. I need a contract for six months.
18. The house is close to the city center.
19. Can I have the key after signing the contract?
20. I don't like the location; it's too crowded.

Chapter 23

Talking About the Past

Key Vocabulary:

Arabic	Pronunciation	Translation
كان	Kān	Was/Were
ذهبت	Dhahabt	I went
رأيت	Ra᾽ayt	I saw
فعلت	Fa῾alt	I did
درست	Darast	I studied
عملت	῾Amilt	I worked
أكلت	᾽Akalt	I ate
شربت	Sharibt	I drank
سافرت	Sāfart	I traveled
قضيت	Qaḍayt	I spent
التقيت	Al-taqayt	I met
شاهدت	Shāhadat	I watched
لعبت	La῾ibt	I played
اشتريت	Ishtarāyt	I bought
أحببت	᾽Aḥbabt	I loved
زرت	Zurt	I visited
كنت	Kunta/Kunti	You were (m/f)
ذهب	Dhahaba	He went
قالت	Qālat	She said
قرأت	Qara᾽t	I read
أمس	᾽Ams	Yesterday
الأسبوع الماضي	Al-᾽Usbū῾ al-māḍī	Last week
السنة الماضية	Al-sanah al-māḍiyah	Last year

Dialogue 1: Talking About a Past Experience

Scenario: Two friends are talking about their past experiences at school.

Arabic: كيف كانت المدرسة معك في الماضي؟
Pronunciation: Kayfa kānat al-madrasah maʿak fī al-māḍī?
Translation: How was school for you in the past?

Arabic: كانت المدرسة جيدة، درست اللغة العربية والرياضيات.
Pronunciation: Kānat al-madrasah jayidah, darastu al-lughah al-ʿArabiyyah wa-al-riyāḍiyāt.
Translation: School was good; I studied Arabic and mathematics.

Arabic: ماذا فعلت بعد المدرسة؟
Pronunciation: Mādhā faʿalta baʿda al-madrasah?
Translation: What did you do after school?

Arabic: بعد المدرسة، عملت في متجر صغير.
Pronunciation: Baʿda al-madrasah, ʿamilt fī matjar ṣaghīr.
Translation: After school, I worked at a small shop.

Arabic: هل أحببت العمل هناك؟
Pronunciation: Hal ʾaḥbabt al-ʿamal hunāk?
Translation: Did you like working there?

Arabic: نعم، أحببت العمل، وتعلمت الكثير.
Pronunciation: Naʿam, ʾaḥbabt al-ʿamal, wa-taʿallamt al-kathīr.
Translation: Yes, I liked the work, and I learned a lot.

Dialogue 2: Describing a Trip

Scenario: A person describes their recent trip to a friend.

Arabic: أين ذهبت في العطلة الماضية؟
Pronunciation: ʾAyna dhahabta fī al-ʿuṭlah al-māḍiyah?
Translation: Where did you go on your last vacation?

Arabic: ذهبت إلى مصر وزرت الأهرامات.
Pronunciation: Dhahabtu ʾilā Miṣr wa-zurt al-ʾahrāmāt.
Translation: I went to Egypt and visited the pyramids.

Arabic: كيف كان الطقس هناك؟
Pronunciation: Kayfa kāna al-ṭaqs hunāk?
Translation: How was the weather there?

Arabic: كان الطقس مشمسًا وحارًا جدًا.
Pronunciation: Kāna al-ṭaqs mushmisan wa-ḥārran jiddan.
Translation: The weather was sunny and very hot.

Arabic: ماذا فعلت في المساء؟
Pronunciation: Mādhā faʿalta fī al-masāʾ?
Translation: What did you do in the evening?

Arabic: في المساء، تناولت العشاء في مطعم محلي.
Pronunciation: Fī al-masāʾ, tanāwalt al-ʿashāʾ fī maṭʿam maḥallī.
Translation: In the evening, I had dinner at a local restaurant.

Arabic: هل اشتريت شيئًا من هناك؟
Pronunciation: Hal ishtarāyta shay'an min hunāk?
Translation: Did you buy anything from there?

Arabic: نعم، اشتريت هدية لأمي.
Pronunciation: Naʿam, ishtarāyt hadīyah li-ummī.
Translation: Yes, I bought a gift for my mother.

Dialogue 3: Recalling Childhood Memories

Scenario: A person is recalling their childhood memories.

Arabic: هل تتذكر طفولتك؟
Pronunciation: Hal tatazakkar ṭufūlatak?
Translation: Do you remember your childhood?

Arabic: نعم، أتذكر الكثير من الأشياء.
Pronunciation: Naʿam, 'atazakkar al-kathīr min al-ashyā'.
Translation: Yes, I remember many things.

Arabic: ماذا كنت تفعل في وقت الفراغ؟
Pronunciation: Mādhā kunta tafʿal fī waqt al-farāgh?
Translation: What did you do in your free time?

Arabic: كنت ألعب في الحديقة مع أصدقائي.
Pronunciation: Kuntu 'alʿab fī al-ḥadīqah maʿa 'aṣdiqā'ī.
Translation: I used to play in the park with my friends.

Arabic: هل كنت تسافر مع عائلتك؟
Pronunciation: Hal kunta tusāfir maʿa ʿā'ilatak?
Translation: Did you travel with your family?

Arabic: نعم، كنا نسافر كل صيف إلى البحر.
Pronunciation: Naʿam, kunnā nusāfir kull ṣayf ʾilā al-baḥr.
Translation: Yes, we traveled every summer to the sea.

Arabic: ماذا كنت تحب أن تأكل؟
Pronunciation: Mādhā kunta tuḥibb ʾan taʾkul?
Translation: What did you like to eat?

Arabic: كنت أحب الأيس كريم والفواكه.
Pronunciation: Kuntu ʾuḥibb al-ʾays krīm wa-al-fawākih.
Translation: I loved ice cream and fruits.

Exercise:

Translate the following sentences into Arabic

1. I went to the market yesterday.
2. We studied English last year.
3. He traveled to France last month.
4. She worked in a restaurant last summer.
5. I met my friends last week.
6. We ate at a new restaurant.
7. They played football in the park.
8. I watched a movie with my family.
9. He saw a beautiful place in the city.
10. I loved visiting my grandparents.
11. She read a book about history.
12. We drank coffee in the morning.
13. They bought gifts for their children.
14. I spent time with my cousin.
15. We enjoyed our trip to the mountains.

16. He did his homework before dinner.
17. She cooked dinner for the family.
18. I watched the sunset at the beach.
19. We visited the museum last weekend.
20. I studied Arabic when I was in school.

Chapter 24

Future Plans and Goals

Key Vocabulary:

Arabic	Pronunciation	Translation
سوف	Sawfa	Will/Going to
أريد	ʾUrīd	I want
سأعمل	Saʾaʿmal	I will work
سأدرس	Saʾadrus	I will study
سأذهب	Saʾadhhab	I will go
سأزور	Saʾazūr	I will visit
سأتعلم	Saʾataʿallam	I will learn
سأشتري	Saʾashtarī	I will buy
سأعيش	Saʾaʿīsh	I will live
سأبدأ	Saʾabdaʾ	I will start
سأكون	Saʾakūn	I will be
أطمح	ʾAṭmaḥ	I aspire
أرغب	ʾArghab	I desire
المستقبل	Al-mustaqbal	The future
أخطط	ʾUkhattiṭ	I plan
الهدف	Al-hadaf	The goal
سأحاول	Saʾuḥāwil	I will try
سأقوم	Saʾaqūm	I will do
قريبًا	Qarīban	Soon
لاحقًا	Lāḥiqan	Later
الأسبوع القادم	Al-ʾusbūʿ al-qādim	Next week

Arabic	Pronunciation	Translation
الشهر القادم	Al-shahr al-qādim	Next month
السنة القادمة	Al-sanah al-qādimah	Next year

Dialogue 1: Discussing Career Goals

Scenario: Two friends are discussing their career plans for the future.

Arabic: ماذا تريد أن تفعل في المستقبل؟
Pronunciation: Mādhā turīd ʾan tafʿal fī al-mustaqbal?
Translation: What do you want to do in the future?

Arabic: أريد أن أعمل كمهندس.
Pronunciation: ʾUrīd ʾan ʾaʿmal ka-muhandis.
Translation: I want to work as an engineer.

Arabic: هل تخطط للدراسة أكثر؟
Pronunciation: Hal tukhaṭṭiṭ lil-dirāsah akthar?
Translation: Do you plan to study more?

Arabic: نعم، سأدرس في الجامعة العام القادم.
Pronunciation: Naʿam, saʾadrus fī al-jāmiʿah al-ʿām al-qādim.
Translation: Yes, I will study at the university next year.

Arabic: وما هو هدفك النهائي؟
Pronunciation: Wa mā huwa hadafak al-nihāʾī?
Translation: And what is your ultimate goal?

Arabic: هدفي أن أكون مديرًا في شركة كبيرة.
Pronunciation: Hadafī ʾan ʾakūn mudīran fī sharikah kabīrah.
Translation: My goal is to be a manager in a big company.

Dialogue 2: Future Travel Plans

Scenario: A person shares their travel plans with a friend.

Arabic: هل تخطط للسفر قريبًا؟
Pronunciation: Hal tukhaṭṭiṭ lil-safar qarīban?
Translation: Are you planning to travel soon?

Arabic: نعم، سأذهب إلى فرنسا الشهر القادم.
Pronunciation: Naʿam, saʾadhhab ʾilā Faransā al-shahr al-qādim.
Translation: Yes, I will go to France next month.

Arabic: ماذا ستفعل هناك؟
Pronunciation: Mādhā sa-tafʿal hunāk?
Translation: What will you do there?

Arabic: سأزور المتاحف وأستمتع بالمدينة.
Pronunciation: Saʾazūr al-matāḥif wa-astamtiʿ bil-madīnah.
Translation: I will visit museums and enjoy the city.

Arabic: هل ستسافر مع العائلة؟
Pronunciation: Hal sa-tusāfir maʿa al-ʿāʾilah?
Translation: Will you travel with your family?

Arabic: لا، سأذهب وحدي لأستكشف المكان.
Pronunciation: Lā, sa'adhhab waḥdī li-astakshif al-makān.
Translation: No, I will go alone to explore the place.

Dialogue 3: Personal Goals and Learning
Scenario: A person talks about their learning goals.

Arabic: هل تنوي تعلم شيء جديد؟
Pronunciation: Hal tanwī ta'allum shay' jadīd?
Translation: Do you intend to learn something new?

Arabic: نعم، سأتعلم اللغة الإسبانية قريبًا.
Pronunciation: Na'am, sa'ata'allam al-lughah al-'Isbānīyah qarīban.
Translation: Yes, I will learn Spanish soon.

Arabic: لماذا تريد تعلمها؟
Pronunciation: Limādhā turīd ta'allumuhā?
Translation: Why do you want to learn it?

Arabic: أريد السفر إلى إسبانيا والعمل هناك.
Pronunciation: 'Urīd al-safar 'ilā 'Isbānīyah wa-al-'amal hunāk.
Translation: I want to travel to Spain and work there.

Arabic: هل تخطط لبدء الدراسة هذا الأسبوع؟
Pronunciation: Hal tukhaṭṭiṭ li-bad' al-dirāsah hādhā al-'usbū'?
Translation: Are you planning to start studying this week?

Arabic: نعم، سأبدأ غدًا بالدروس الأولى.
Pronunciation: Naʿam, saʾabdaʾ ghadan bil-durūs al-ʾūlā.
Translation: Yes, I will start tomorrow with the first lessons.

Exercise:

Translate the following sentences into Arabic

1. I will study at the university next year.
2. We will travel to Italy next summer.
3. She will learn French because she wants to work there.
4. I plan to buy a new car next month.
5. They will start their new jobs next week.
6. I will be a doctor in the future.
7. He will work in a big company soon.
8. We will visit our grandparents next weekend.
9. She will try to learn cooking this year.
10. I aspire to be an artist in the future.
11. We want to live in a new house.
12. I will go to the gym tomorrow.
13. He plans to start his own business next year.
14. I will watch the new movie next Friday.
15. She will read a book this weekend.
16. We will meet our friends next Saturday.
17. I will try to learn a new skill next month.
18. He will travel to Japan next winter.
19. I want to be fluent in Arabic.
20. We will go shopping next week.

Chapter 25

Discussing Education and Schools

Key Vocabulary:

Arabic	Pronunciation	Translation
مدرسة	Madrasa	School
جامعة	Jāmiʿa	University
طالب	Ṭālib	Student (male)
طالبة	Ṭālibah	Student (female)
معلم	Muʿallim	Teacher (male)
معلمة	Muʿallimah	Teacher (female)
دراسة	Dirāsah	Study/Studies
صف	Ṣaff	Class
امتحان	Imtiḥān	Exam
واجب	Wājib	Homework
مادة	Māddah	Subject
الرياضيات	Al-Riyāḍiyyāt	Mathematics
العلوم	Al-ʿUlūm	Science
اللغة العربية	Al-Lughah al-ʿArabiyyah	Arabic Language
تاريخ	Tārīkh	History
تخرج	Takharruj	Graduation
شهادة	Shahādah	Certificate/Degree
فصل دراسي	Faṣl Dirāsī	Semester
مكتبة	Maktabah	Library
زميل	Zamīl	Classmate (male)
زميلة	Zamīlah	Classmate (female)

Arabic	Pronunciation	Translation
قاعة دراسية	Qāʿah Dirāsīyah	Classroom
مستوى	Mustawā	Level
دراسة جامعية	Dirāsah Jāmiʿīyah	University Study
حلم	Ḥulm	Dream

Dialogue 1: Discussing School Life

Scenario: Two students are talking about their school routine.

Arabic: كيف تجد المدرسة؟
Pronunciation: Kayfa tajid al-madrasa?
Translation: How do you find school?

Arabic: أحب المدرسة كثيرًا، وخاصة مادة العلوم.
Pronunciation: ʾUḥibb al-madrasa kathīran, wa-khāṣṣatan māddat al-ʿulūm.
Translation: I love school a lot, especially Science.

Arabic: ومن هو معلمك المفضل؟
Pronunciation: Wa man huwa muʿallimuk al-mufaḍḍal?
Translation: And who is your favorite teacher?

Arabic: معلم الرياضيات، هو معلم رائع.
Pronunciation: Muʿallim al-riyāḍiyyāt, huwa muʿallim rāʾiʿ.
Translation: The Math teacher; he is amazing.

Arabic: وهل تحب الدراسة في المكتبة؟
Pronunciation: Wa hal tuḥibb al-dirāsah fī al-maktabah?
Translation: Do you like studying in the library?

Arabic: نعم، أحب الهدوء هناك.
Pronunciation: Naʿam, ʾuḥibb al-hudūʾ hunāk.
Translation: Yes, I like the quiet there.

Dialogue 2: Discussing Future Studies

Scenario: Two friends discuss their future academic goals.

Arabic: ماذا تخطط للدراسة بعد المدرسة؟
Pronunciation: Mādhā tukhaṭṭiṭ lil-dirāsah baʿd al-madrasa?
Translation: What do you plan to study after school?

Arabic: سأدرس في الجامعة وأريد أن أكون طبيبًا.
Pronunciation: Saʾadrus fī al-jāmiʿah wa-ʾurīd ʾan ʾakūn ṭabīban.
Translation: I will study at the university and want to become a doctor.

Arabic: رائع! وأنا سأدرس الهندسة.
Pronunciation: Rāʾiʿ! Wa-ʾanā saʾadrus al-handasah.
Translation: Great! And I will study engineering.

Arabic: هل تخطط للدراسة في الخارج؟
Pronunciation: Hal tukhaṭṭiṭ lil-dirāsah fī al-khārij?
Translation: Are you planning to study abroad?

Arabic: نعم، أريد أن أحصل على شهادة دولية.
Pronunciation: Naʿam, ʾurīd ʾan ʾaḥṣul ʿalā shahādah duwalīyah.
Translation: Yes, I want to get an international degree.

Arabic: أتمنى لك التوفيق في المستقبل!
Pronunciation: ʾAtamannā laka al-tawfīq fī al-mustaqbal!
Translation: I wish you success in the future!

Dialogue 3: Classroom Discussion

Scenario: A teacher asks students about their favorite subjects.

Arabic: ما هي مادتك المفضلة؟
Pronunciation: Mā hiya māddatuk al-mufaḍḍalah?
Translation: What is your favorite subject?

Arabic: أحب اللغة العربية لأنها لغة جميلة.
Pronunciation: ʾUḥibb al-lughah al-ʿArabiyyah li-ʾannahā lughah jamīlah.
Translation: I love the Arabic language because it's a beautiful language.

Arabic: وأنا أحب التاريخ لأنه ممتع.
Pronunciation: Wa ʾanā ʾuḥibb al-tārīkh li-ʾannahū mumtiʿ.
Translation: And I love history because it's interesting.

Arabic: كيف تستعد للامتحانات؟
Pronunciation: Kayfa tastaʿidd lil-imtiḥānāt?
Translation: How do you prepare for exams?

Arabic: أدرس بجد وأراجع في المكتبة.
Pronunciation: ʾAdrusu bi-jidd wa-ʾurājiʿ fī al-maktabah.
Translation: I study hard and review in the library.

Arabic: هل تقوم بالواجبات يوميًا؟
Pronunciation: Hal taqūm bil-wājibāt yawmiyan?
Translation: Do you do your homework daily?

Arabic: نعم، الواجبات تساعدني في الفهم.
Pronunciation: Naʿam, al-wājibāt tusāʿidunī fī al-fahm.
Translation: Yes, homework helps me understand.

Exercise:

Translate the following sentences into Arabic

1. I want to study at the university.
2. My favorite subject is Science.
3. The teacher is very good and helpful.
4. I will do my homework after class.
5. We have an exam next week.
6. I study at school every day.
7. My classmate is very friendly.
8. I want to get a degree in engineering.
9. The library is a quiet place for studying.
10. I have a history exam tomorrow.
11. I plan to study abroad after graduation.
12. Our Math teacher is very strict.
13. I want to improve my Arabic language skills.
14. The classroom is big and bright.
15. I have a dream to become a doctor.
16. I need to prepare for my final exams.
17. The school has a large library.
18. I love my school because the teachers are great.
19. I need to review my lessons today.
20. My friend will study Science next semester.

Chapter 26

Talking About Transportation

Key Vocabulary:

Arabic	Pronunciation	Translation
سيارة	Sayyārah	Car
حافلة	Ḥāfilah	Bus
قطار	Qiṭār	Train
طائرة	Ṭā'irah	Airplane
دراجة	Dirājah	Bicycle
دراجة نارية	Dirājah Nārīyah	Motorcycle
تاكسي	Tāksī	Taxi
محطة	Maḥaṭṭah	Station
مطار	Maṭār	Airport
تذكرة	Tadhkirah	Ticket
رحلة	Riḥlah	Trip/Flight
طريق	Ṭarīq	Road
مزدحم	Muzdaḥim	Crowded
سريع	Sarī'	Fast
بطيء	Baṭī'	Slow
موقف	Mawqif	Stop
اتجاه	Ittiḥāh	Direction
يمين	Yamīn	Right
يسار	Yasār	Left
وسط المدينة	Wasaṭ al-Madīnah	City Center
خريطة	Kharīṭah	Map
ساعة الذروة	Sā'at al-Dhurwah	Rush Hour

Arabic	Pronunciation	Translation
الوصول	Al-Wuṣūl	Arrival
المغادرة	Al-Mughādara	Departure
سائق	Sā'iq	Driver
ركوب	Rukūb	Riding
مشي	Mashī	Walking
حزام الأمان	Ḥizām al-Amān	Seatbelt
تذاكر	Tadhākir	Tickets

Dialogue 1: Asking About Transportation Options

Scenario: Two friends are discussing their options for going to the city center.

Arabic: كيف نذهب إلى وسط المدينة؟
Pronunciation: Kayfa nadhhab 'ilā wasaṭ al-madīnah?
Translation: How do we get to the city center?

Arabic: يمكننا ركوب الحافلة أو القطار.
Pronunciation: Yumkinunā rukūb al-ḥāfilah 'aw al-qiṭār.
Translation: We can take the bus or the train.

Arabic: أيهما أسرع؟
Pronunciation: 'Ayyuhumā asra'?
Translation: Which one is faster?

Arabic: القطار أسرع بكثير، ولكنه مزدحم في ساعة الذروة.
Pronunciation: Al-qiṭār asra' bikaṯīr, walākinahu muzdaḥim fī sā'at al-dhurwah.
Translation: The train is much faster, but it's crowded during rush hour.

Arabic: وما هي تكلفة التذكرة؟
Pronunciation: Wa mā hiya taklīfat al-tadhkirah?
Translation: And what is the cost of the ticket?

Arabic: تذكرة القطار أغلى قليلاً من الحافلة.
Pronunciation: Tadhkirat al-qiṭār aghlā qalīlan min al-ḥāfilah.
Translation: The train ticket is a little more expensive than the bus.

Dialogue 2: Asking for Directions to the Station

Scenario: A tourist is asking for directions to the train station.

Arabic: من فضلك، أين تقع محطة القطار؟
Pronunciation: Min faḍlik, ʾayna taqaʿ maḥaṭṭat al-qiṭār?
Translation: Excuse me, where is the train station?

Arabic: امشِ مستقيمًا، ثم انعطف يمينًا عند الإشارة.
Pronunciation: Imshī mustaqīman, thumma inʿaṭif yamīnan ʿind al-ishārah.
Translation: Walk straight, then turn right at the traffic light.

Arabic: وهل هي بعيدة؟
Pronunciation: Wa hal hiya baʿīdah?
Translation: Is it far?

Arabic: ليست بعيدة، حوالي عشر دقائق مشيًا.
Pronunciation: Laysat baʿīdah, ḥawālī ʿashar daqāʾiq mashyan.
Translation: It's not far, about ten minutes walking.

Arabic: شكرًا جزيلاً!
Pronunciation: Shukran jazīlan!
Translation: Thank you very much!

Arabic: على الرحب والسعة!
Pronunciation: ʿAlā al-raḥb wa al-saʿah!
Translation: You're welcome!

Dialogue 3: At the Taxi Stand

Scenario: A passenger is speaking with a taxi driver.

Arabic: هل يمكنك أن تأخذني إلى المطار؟
Pronunciation: Hal yumkinuka ʾan taʾkhudhni ʾilā al-maṭār?
Translation: Can you take me to the airport?

Arabic: نعم، بالتأكيد. متى موعد رحلتك؟
Pronunciation: Naʿam, bi-al-taʾkīd. Matā mawʿid riḥlatik?
Translation: Yes, of course. When is your flight?

Arabic: رحلتي في الساعة الخامسة مساءً.
Pronunciation: Riḥlatī fī al-sāʿah al-khāmisah masāʾan.
Translation: My flight is at five in the evening.

Arabic: سنصل في حوالي نصف ساعة.
Pronunciation: Sanaṣil fī ḥawālī niṣf sāʿah.
Translation: We will arrive in about half an hour.

Arabic: هل لديك حزام الأمان؟
Pronunciation: Hal ladayka ḥizām al-amān?
Translation: Do you have a seatbelt?

Arabic: نعم، تأكد من ربطه من فضلك.
Pronunciation: Naʿam, taʾakkad min rabṭihi min faḍlik.
Translation: Yes, please make sure to fasten it.

Exercise:

Translate the following sentences into Arabic

1. I want to go to the city center by bus.
2. The train is fast but sometimes crowded.
3. Where can I buy a ticket for the bus?
4. My flight departs from the airport at 8 AM.
5. The taxi is waiting at the hotel.
6. How much is the ticket to the train station?
7. The bus stop is near my house.
8. I prefer to ride a bicycle in the city.
9. The traffic is heavy during rush hour.
10. Is the taxi expensive compared to the bus?
11. I usually take the car to work.
12. The bus arrives at the station at 6 PM.
13. I need a map to find the train station.
14. The driver is very polite and helpful.
15. We are walking to the restaurant tonight.
16. The road to the airport is very busy.
17. How long does it take to get to the city center?
18. The motorcycle is faster than walking.
19. I like to travel by airplane for long distances.
20. The train leaves from platform number three.

Chapter 27

Cultural Traditions and Celebrations

Key Vocabulary:

Arabic	Pronunciation	Translation
عيد	ʿĪd	Holiday/Festival
احتفال	Iḥtifāl	Celebration
تقليد	Taqālīd	Tradition
عيد الفطر	ʿĪd al-Fiṭr	Eid al-Fitr
عيد الأضحى	ʿĪd al-Aḍḥā	Eid al-Adha
رمضان	Ramaḍān	Ramadan
حفل	Ḥafl	Party
زفاف	Zafāf	Wedding
ميلاد	Mīlād	Birthday
زينة	Zīnah	Decoration
طعام	Ṭaʿām	Food
تقليدي	Taqālīdī	Traditional
هدية	Hadīyah	Gift
ضيف	Ḍayf	Guest
وليمة	Walīmah	Feast
صلاة	Ṣalāh	Prayer
تهنئة	Tahnīʾah	Congratulations
ملابس تقليدية	Malābis Taqālīdīyah	Traditional Clothes
عيد ميلاد	ʿĪd Mīlād	Birthday
عائلة	ʿĀʾilah	Family
احتفالات	Iḥtifālāt	Celebrations

Arabic	Pronunciation	Translation
مهرجان	Mahrājān	Festival
فطور	Fuṭūr	Breakfast (during Ramadan)
طقوس	Ṭuqūs	Rituals
ثقافة	Thaqāfah	Culture
دعوة	Daʿwah	Invitation
مبارك	Mubārak	Blessed/Congratulation

Dialogue 1: Talking About Eid Celebrations

Scenario: Two friends are discussing how they celebrate Eid.

Arabic: كيف تحتفل بعيد الفطر؟
Pronunciation: Kayfa taḥtafil bi-ʿĪd al-Fiṭr?
Translation: How do you celebrate Eid al-Fitr?

Arabic: نذهب إلى المسجد ونصلي صلاة العيد.
Pronunciation: Nadhhab ʾilā al-masjid wa nuṣallī ṣalāt al-ʿĪd.
Translation: We go to the mosque and perform the Eid prayer.

Arabic: ثم نتناول الفطور مع العائلة ونقدم الهدايا للأطفال.
Pronunciation: Thumma natanāwul al-fuṭūr maʿ al-ʿāʾilah wa nuqaddim al-hadāyā lil-aṭfāl.
Translation: Then we have breakfast with the family and give gifts to the children.

Arabic: هل تلبس ملابس تقليدية في العيد؟
Pronunciation: Hal talbis malābis taqālīdīyah fī al-ʿĪd?
Translation: Do you wear traditional clothes on Eid?

Arabic: نعم، نرتدي الثياب الجديدة ونزور الأقارب والأصدقاء.
Pronunciation: Naʿam, nartadī al-thiyāb al-jadīdah wa nazūr al-aqārib wa al-aṣdiqāʾ.
Translation: Yes, we wear new clothes and visit relatives and friends.

Dialogue 2: Discussing a Wedding Invitation

Scenario: A friend invites another to attend a wedding.

Arabic: مرحبًا، هل تود حضور حفل زفافي؟
Pronunciation: Marḥabān, hal tawadd ḥuḍūr ḥafl zafāfī?
Translation: Hello, would you like to attend my wedding?

Arabic: نعم، بالطبع! متى موعد الحفل؟
Pronunciation: Naʿam, bi-al-ṭabʿ! Matā mawʿid al-ḥafl?
Translation: Yes, of course! When is the wedding?

Arabic: الحفل يوم الجمعة القادم في الساعة السابعة مساءً.
Pronunciation: Al-ḥafl yawm al-jumʿah al-qādim fī al-sāʿah al-sābiʿah masāʾan.
Translation: The wedding is next Friday at 7 PM.

Arabic: سأكون هناك بالتأكيد! هل تحتاج مساعدة في التحضير؟
Pronunciation: Saʾakūn hunāk bi-al-taʾkīd! Hal taḥtāj musāʿadah fī al-taḥḍīr?
Translation: I'll definitely be there! Do you need help with the preparations?

Arabic: شكرًا جزيلاً، الأمور مرتبة. فقط أحضر نفسك واستمتع بالحفل.
Pronunciation: Shukran jazīlan, al-umūr murattabah. Faqaṭ aḥḍir nafsak wa istamti' bi-al-ḥafl.
Translation: Thank you very much, everything is arranged. Just bring yourself and enjoy the party.

Dialogue 3: Describing a Cultural Festival

Scenario: Two friends discuss a cultural festival they attended.

Arabic: كيف كان مهرجان الثقافة البارحة؟
Pronunciation: Kayfa kān mahrājān al-thaqāfah al-bāriḥah?
Translation: How was the cultural festival yesterday?

Arabic: كان رائعًا! كان هناك الكثير من الطقوس التقليدية والأطعمة الشهية.
Pronunciation: Kāna rā'i'an! Kāna hunāk al-kathīr min al-ṭuqūs al-taqālīdīyah wa al-aṭ'imah al-shahīyah.
Translation: It was amazing! There were many traditional rituals and delicious foods.

Arabic: هل كان هناك عرض للملابس التقليدية؟
Pronunciation: Hal kān hunāk 'arḍ lil-malābis al-taqālīdīyah?
Translation: Was there a display of traditional clothes?

Arabic: نعم، وكان الناس يرتدون ملابس ملونة وجميلة.
Pronunciation: Na'am, wa kān al-nās yartadūn malābis malawnah wa jamīlah.
Translation: Yes, and people were wearing colorful and beautiful clothes.

Arabic: هل حضر الكثير من الناس؟
Pronunciation: Hal ḥaḍar al-kathīr min al-nās?
Translation: Did many people attend?

Arabic: نعم، كان المهرجان مزدحمًا بالزوار.
Pronunciation: Naʿam, kān al-mahrājān muzdaḥimān bi-al-zawwār.
Translation: Yes, the festival was crowded with visitors.

Exercise:

Translate the following sentences into Arabic

1. We celebrate Eid with family and friends.
2. The wedding will be on Sunday evening.
3. My birthday is in the summer.
4. Traditional clothes are worn during festivals.
5. The cultural festival had delicious food and music.
6. Congratulations on your new job!
7. We visited our relatives during the holiday.
8. The decorations at the party were beautiful.
9. I received a gift from my friend.
10. Do you like traditional celebrations?
11. The guest brought a lovely gift to the house.
12. The family gathered for a large feast.
13. Ramadan is a month of fasting and prayer.
14. We light candles during the celebration.
15. The holiday traditions are very important to us.
16. The wedding had many traditional rituals.
17. I sent an invitation to all my friends.
18. The food at the festival was amazing.
19. I enjoy learning about different cultures.
20. The party starts at 7 PM on Friday.

Chapter 28
Business Arabic

Key Vocabulary:

Arabic	Pronunciation	Translation
عمل	ʿAmal	Work/Job
شركة	Sharikah	Company
اجتماع	Ijtimāʿ	Meeting
وظيفة	Waẓīfah	Job/Position
مدير	Mudīr	Manager
موظف	Muwaẓẓaf	Employee
مشروع	Mashrūʿ	Project
عقد	ʿAqd	Contract
راتب	Rātib	Salary
فريق	Farīq	Team
منتج	Muntaj	Product
خدمة	Khidmah	Service
مبيعات	Mabīʿāt	Sales
تسويق	Taswīq	Marketing
تفاوض	Tafāwuḍ	Negotiation
عميل	ʿAmīl	Client/Customer
سوق	Sūq	Market
تقرير	Taqrīr	Report
موعد	Mawʿid	Appointment
استثمار	Istithmār	Investment
عرض	ʿArḍ	Presentation/Offer
تعاون	Taʿāwun	Collaboration

Arabic	Pronunciation	Translation
هدف	Hadaf	Goal
خطة	Khiṭṭah	Plan
ميزانية	Mīzānīyah	Budget
اتفاق	Ittifāq	Agreement
صفقة	Ṣafqah	Deal
مورد	Mawrid	Supplier
تقرير	Taqrīr	Report
موعد نهائي	Mawʿid Nihāʾī	Deadline

Dialogue 1: Setting Up a Business Meeting

Scenario: An employee arranges a meeting with their manager.

Arabic: مرحبًا، هل يمكننا ترتيب اجتماع لمناقشة المشروع الجديد؟
Pronunciation: Marḥabān, hal yumkinunā tartīb ijtimāʿ li-munāqashat al-mashrūʿ al-jadīd?
Translation: Hello, can we arrange a meeting to discuss the new project?

Arabic: بالتأكيد، ما هو الوقت المناسب لك؟
Pronunciation: Bi-al-taʾkīd, mā huwa al-waqt al-munāsib lak?
Translation: Certainly, what time suits you?

Arabic: يوم الثلاثاء في الساعة العاشرة صباحًا.
Pronunciation: Yawm al-thulāthāʾ fī al-sāʿah al-ʿāshirah ṣabāḥan.
Translation: Tuesday at 10 AM.

Arabic: ممتاز، سأرسل لك دعوة الاجتماع عبر البريد الإلكتروني.
Pronunciation: Mumtāz, sa'ursil lak da'wah al-ijtimā' 'abra al-barīd al-'iliktirūnī.
Translation: Great, I'll send you the meeting invitation via email.

Arabic: شكرًا، سأحضر التقرير عن المشروع.
Pronunciation: Shukran, sa'aḥḍur al-taqrīr 'an al-mashrū'.
Translation: Thank you, I will bring the report about the project.

Dialogue 2: Discussing a Contract with a Client

Scenario: A manager and a client negotiate a contract.

Arabic: مرحبًا، لنبدأ بمناقشة تفاصيل العقد.
Pronunciation: Marḥabān, linabdā' bi-munāqashat tafāṣīl al-'aqd.
Translation: Hello, let's start discussing the contract details.

Arabic: نعم، نحتاج إلى معرفة مدة العقد والتكاليف.
Pronunciation: Na'am, naḥtāj 'ilā ma'rifah muddat al-'aqd wa al-takālīf.
Translation: Yes, we need to know the contract duration and costs.

Arabic: العقد سيكون لمدة سنة، والتكلفة ستكون خمسة آلاف دولار شهريًا.
Pronunciation: Al-ʿaqd sayakūn li-muddah sanah, wa al-taklīfah sayakūn khamsah ālāf dūlār shahrīyan.
Translation: The contract will be for one year, and the cost will be five thousand dollars per month.

Arabic: هل يمكننا مراجعة الميزانية قبل التوقيع؟
Pronunciation: Hal yumkinunā murājaʿah al-mīzānīyah qabl al-tawqīʿ?
Translation: Can we review the budget before signing?

Arabic: بالطبع، سأرسل لك الميزانية غدًا.
Pronunciation: Bi-al-ṭabʿ, saʾursil lak al-mīzānīyah ghadān.
Translation: Of course, I will send you the budget tomorrow.

Arabic: شكرًا، نأمل أن نتعاون بشكل جيد.
Pronunciation: Shukran, naʾmal ʾan nataʿāwan bi-shakl jayid.
Translation: Thank you, we hope to collaborate well.

Dialogue 3: Presenting a Business Proposal

Scenario: An employee presents a business proposal to their team.

Arabic: اليوم، سأقدم عرضًا عن خطة التسويق للمشروع الجديد.
Pronunciation: Al-yawm, saʾuqaddim ʿarḍan ʿan khiṭṭat al-taswīq li-al-mashrūʿ al-jadīd.
Translation: Today, I will present a marketing plan for the new project.

Arabic: ما هو الهدف الرئيسي من هذه الخطة؟
Pronunciation: Mā huwa al-hadaf al-raʾīsī min hādhihi al-khiṭṭah?
Translation: What is the main goal of this plan?

Arabic: الهدف هو زيادة المبيعات بنسبة عشرين بالمائة خلال ستة أشهر.
Pronunciation: Al-hadaf huwa zīyādah al-mabīʿāt bi-nisbah ʿishrīn bil-mīʾah khilāl sittah ashhur.
Translation: The goal is to increase sales by 20% within six months.

Arabic: ما هي الاستراتيجية لتحقيق هذا الهدف؟
Pronunciation: Mā hiya al-istirātījīyah li-taḥqīq hādhā al-hadaf?
Translation: What is the strategy to achieve this goal?

Arabic: سنركز على التسويق الرقمي وتعزيز العلاقات مع العملاء.
Pronunciation: Sana-rakkiz ʿalā al-taswīq al-raqamī wa taʿzīz al-ʿalāqāt maʿ al-ʿumlāʾ.
Translation: We will focus on digital marketing and strengthening relationships with clients.

Arabic: جيد، هل هناك أي ميزانية إضافية مطلوبة؟
Pronunciation: Jayid, hal hunāk ay mīzānīyah ʾiḍāfīyah maṭlūbah?
Translation: Good, is there any additional budget required?

Arabic: نعم، نحتاج إلى عشرة آلاف دولار لتغطية الإعلانات.
Pronunciation: Naʿam, naḥtāj ʾilā ʿashrah ālāf dūlār li-taghṭiyah al-iʿlānāt.
Translation: Yes, we need ten thousand dollars for advertising.

Arabic: سننظر في الأمر، ولكن الخطة تبدو جيدة حتى الآن.
Pronunciation: Sananẓur fī al-ʾamr, walākin al-khiṭṭah tabdū jayidah ḥattá al-ān.
Translation: We will look into it, but the plan looks good so far.

Exercise:

Translate the following sentences into Arabic

1. We need to schedule a meeting with the manager.
2. The company is launching a new product next month.
3. The employee is preparing a report on the project.
4. We have a meeting with the client tomorrow.
5. The contract needs to be signed before the deadline.
6. The team is working on the new marketing plan.
7. Our goal is to increase sales by 20%.
8. The manager will present the project to the team.
9. The budget for this plan needs to be reviewed.
10. We will discuss the details of the contract today.
11. The company is looking for a new employee.
12. The salary for this position is very competitive.
13. Our team is collaborating on this project.
14. The client agreed to the terms of the agreement.
15. We have a deadline to complete this task.
16. The business proposal will be presented next week.

17. The supplier is providing the materials for the project.
18. The employee is responsible for the sales report.
19. We need to arrange an appointment with the client.
20. The manager is reviewing the budget for the project.

Chapter 29

Problems and Complaints

Key Vocabulary:

Arabic	Pronunciation	Translation
مشكلة	Mushkilah	Problem
شكوى	Shakwā	Complaint
غير مقبول	Ghayr Maqbūl	Unacceptable
خطأ	Khaṭaʾ	Mistake/Error
تأخير	Taʾkhīr	Delay
خدمة	Khidmah	Service
إصلاح	Iṣlāḥ	Repair
معطل	Muʿaṭṭal	Broken
سيء	Sayyiʾ	Bad
تأجيل	Taʾjīl	Postponement
غير راضٍ	Ghayr Rāḍin	Unsatisfied
تذمر	Tadhammur	Complaint/Grievance
مشكلة تقنية	Mushkilah Taqniyyah	Technical problem
إعادة	Iʿādah	Return
تعويض	Taʿwīḍ	Compensation
تصليح	Taṣlīḥ	Fixing/Repair
خطأ في الحساب	Khaṭaʾ fī al-Ḥisāb	Billing error
موعد	Mawʿid	Appointment
جودة	Jawdah	Quality
غير مناسب	Ghayr Munāsib	Inappropriate/Unsuitable

Dialogue 1: Reporting a Problem at a Hotel

Scenario: A guest complains about a problem with their room at the hotel.

Arabic: عذرًا، لدي مشكلة في الغرفة.
Pronunciation: ʿUdhuran, laday mushkilah fī al-ghurfah.
Translation: Excuse me, I have a problem with the room.

Arabic: ما هي المشكلة بالضبط؟
Pronunciation: Mā hiya al-mushkilah bi-al-ḍabṭ?
Translation: What exactly is the problem?

Arabic: التكييف معطل ولا يعمل.
Pronunciation: Al-takyīf muʿaṭṭal walā yaʿmal.
Translation: The air conditioning is broken and not working.

Arabic: نعتذر عن ذلك، سنرسل أحد الفنيين لإصلاحه.
Pronunciation: Naʿtadhir ʿan dhālik, sanursil aḥad al-fanniyīn li-iṣlāḥih.
Translation: We apologize for that; we will send a technician to fix it.

Arabic: شكرًا، أرجو أن يتم ذلك بسرعة.
Pronunciation: Shukran, arjū ʾan yatim dhālik bi-surʿah.
Translation: Thank you, please make it quick.

Dialogue 2: Making a Complaint About a Product
Scenario: A customer complains about a defective product they bought.

Arabic: اشتريت هذا المنتج، لكنه معطل.
Pronunciation: Ishtarayt hādhā al-muntaj, lākinnahu mu'aṭṭal.
Translation: I bought this product, but it's defective.

Arabic: نعتذر عن الإزعاج، هل لديك الفاتورة؟
Pronunciation: Na'tadhir 'an al-iz'āj, hal ladayk al-fātūrah?
Translation: We apologize for the inconvenience, do you have the receipt?

Arabic: نعم، وهذه هي الفاتورة.
Pronunciation: Na'am, wa-hādhihi hiya al-fātūrah.
Translation: Yes, here is the receipt.

Arabic: يمكنك استبدال المنتج أو استرداد المال.
Pronunciation: Yumkinuka istibdāl al-muntaj aw istirād al-māl.
Translation: You can either exchange the product or get a refund.

Arabic: أود استرداد المال، شكرًا.
Pronunciation: 'Uwad istirād al-māl, shukran.
Translation: I would like a refund, thank you.

Dialogue 3: Complaining About Poor Service at a Restaurant

Scenario: A customer complains about slow service at a restaurant.

Arabic: الخدمة بطيئة جدًا، ونحن ننتظر لأكثر من ساعة.
Pronunciation: Al-khidmah baṭīʾah jiddan, wa-naḥnu nantaẓir li-ʾakthar min sāʿah.
Translation: The service is very slow, and we have been waiting for more than an hour.

Arabic: نعتذر عن التأخير، كان هناك ضغط كبير اليوم.
Pronunciation: Naʿtadhir ʿan al-taʾkhīr, kāna hunāk ḍagṭ kabīr al-yawm.
Translation: We apologize for the delay, it's been very busy today.

Arabic: أتفهم ذلك، لكننا غير راضين عن الخدمة.
Pronunciation: ʾAtfahham dhālik, lākinnā ghayr rāḍīn ʿan al-khidmah.
Translation: I understand, but we are not satisfied with the service.

Arabic: سنتأكد من تحسين الخدمة ونقدم لكم خصمًا على الفاتورة.
Pronunciation: Sanataʾakkad min taḥsīn al-khidmah wa-nuqaddim lakum khaṣman ʿalā al-fātūrah.
Translation: We will ensure better service and offer you a discount on the bill.

Arabic: شكرًا لتفهمك، نأمل أن تكون الخدمة أفضل في المستقبل.
Pronunciation: Shukran li-tafahhumik, naʾmal ʾan takūn al-khidmah ʾafḍal fī al-mustaqbal.
Translation: Thank you for understanding, we hope the service will be better in the future.

Exercise:

Translate the following sentences into Arabic

1. I have a problem with the service; it's unacceptable.
2. The air conditioner is not working; it needs repair.
3. The product is defective; I want a refund.
4. There is a mistake in the bill; can you check it?
5. I am not satisfied with the quality of the food.
6. There was a delay in my order, and I am unhappy.
7. Can I file a complaint about the poor service?
8. I would like to talk to the manager about the problem.
9. The technician came but didn't fix the issue.
10. I need compensation for the delay in service.
11. The room is not clean; this is a big problem.
12. We are not satisfied with the agreement terms.
13. I want to return this item because it's not suitable.
14. There is a technical problem with the system.
15. We need to report this issue to customer service.
16. My flight was postponed; I need to complain.
17. The food is cold, and the service is slow.
18. I received the wrong order; please fix this mistake.
19. Can I speak to someone about this issue?
20. The technician was late, and the problem is still there.

Chapter 30

Reviewing and Celebrating Progress

Key Vocabulary:

Arabic	Pronunciation	Translation
إنجاز	Injāz	Achievement
نجاح	Najāḥ	Success
تقدم	Taqaddum	Progress
فخر	Fakhr	Pride
احتفال	Iḥtifāl	Celebration
شكراً	Shukran	Thank you
مجهود	Majhūd	Effort
تطور	Taṭawwur	Development
أهداف	Ahdāf	Goals
فوز	Fawz	Victory
تحسين	Taḥsīn	Improvement
إصرار	Iṣrār	Determination
تحدي	Taḥaddī	Challenge
شكر	Shukr	Gratitude
متفوق	Mutafawwiq	Outstanding
طموح	Ṭumūḥ	Ambition
تجربة	Tajrubah	Experience
خطوة	Khuṭwah	Step
مسار	Masār	Path
مستقبل	Mustaqbal	Future

Dialogue 1: Discussing Personal Achievements

Scenario: A student talks with their teacher about the progress they have made over the course.

Arabic: أشعر بالفخر لأنني حققت الكثير هذا العام.
Pronunciation: Ashʿur bi-al-fakhr li-ʾannanī ḥaqqaqtu al-kathīr hādhā al-ʿām.
Translation: I feel proud because I achieved a lot this year.

Arabic: هذا إنجاز رائع، كيف شعرت بالتقدم؟
Pronunciation: Hādhā injāz rāʾiʿ, kayfa shaʿarta bi-al-taqaddum?
Translation: This is a great achievement, how did you feel about the progress?

Arabic: في البداية كان التحدي صعباً، ولكن الآن أشعر بالتطور.
Pronunciation: Fī al-bidāyah kāna al-taḥaddī ṣaʿban, walākin al-ʾān ashʿur bi-al-taṭawwur.
Translation: At first, the challenge was hard, but now I feel the development.

Arabic: نعم، لقد بذلت مجهوداً كبيراً وتستحق النجاح.
Pronunciation: Naʿam, laqad badhulta majhūdan kabīran wa-tastaḥiqu al-najāḥ.
Translation: Yes, you have put in a lot of effort and deserve success.

Dialogue 2: Celebrating Team Success

Scenario: A manager celebrates the achievements of their team at work.

Arabic: فريقنا حقق إنجازات عظيمة هذا العام.
Pronunciation: Farīqunā ḥaqqaqa injāzāt ʿaẓīmah hādhā al-ʿām.
Translation: Our team achieved great accomplishments this year.

Arabic: نعم، الجهود المشتركة جعلت هذا ممكناً.
Pronunciation: Naʿam, al-juhūd al-mushtarakah jaʿalat hādhā mumkinan.
Translation: Yes, the joint efforts made this possible.

Arabic: أود أن أشكر الجميع على العمل الجاد.
Pronunciation: ʾUwad ʾan ʾashkur al-jamīʿ ʿalā al-ʿamal al-jād.
Translation: I want to thank everyone for their hard work.

Arabic: دعونا نحتفل بهذا النجاح ونتطلع إلى المزيد.
Pronunciation: Daʿūnā naḥtafil bi-hādhā al-najāḥ wa-natataḷla' ilā al-mazeed.
Translation: Let's celebrate this success and look forward to more.

Arabic: بالتأكيد، معاً يمكننا تحقيق المزيد من الأهداف.
Pronunciation: Bi-al-taʾkīd, maʿan yumkinunā taḥqīq al-mazeed min al-ahdāf.
Translation: Certainly, together we can achieve more goals.

Dialogue 3: Reflecting on Progress with a Friend

Scenario: Two friends discuss their personal growth and future goals.

Arabic: أنا فخور بالخطوات التي اتخذتها هذا العام.
Pronunciation: ʾAnā fakhūr bi-al-khuṭuwāt allatī ittakhadhthuhā hādhā al-ʿām.
Translation: I am proud of the steps I have taken this year.

Arabic: لقد رأيت تطورك وأنت تستحق كل التقدير.
Pronunciation: Laqad raʾaytu taṭawwurak wa-ʾanta tastaḥiq kull al-taqdīr.
Translation: I have seen your progress, and you deserve all the appreciation.

Arabic: أود أن أحقق المزيد في المستقبل.
Pronunciation: ʾUwad ʾan ʾaḥaqīq al-mazeed fī al-mustaqbal.
Translation: I want to achieve more in the future.

Arabic: لا شك في ذلك، مع الإصرار يمكنك الوصول إلى أهدافك.
Pronunciation: Lā shak fī dhālik, maʿa al-iṣrār yumkinuka al-wuṣūl ilā ahdāfik.
Translation: No doubt about it, with determination, you can reach your goals.

Arabic: شكراً لدعمك المستمر، كان له أثر كبير.
Pronunciation: Shukran li-daʿmik al-mustamir, kāna lahu athar kabīr.
Translation: Thank you for your continuous support; it has had a great impact.

Exercise:

Translate the following sentences into Arabic

1. I am proud of my progress this year.
2. Our team achieved great success in the project.
3. We should celebrate our accomplishments together.
4. Your determination helped you overcome challenges.
5. I want to improve my skills in the future.
6. We set our goals and achieved them with effort.
7. Thank you for your support; it made a big difference.
8. We are celebrating the victory of our hard work.
9. Reflecting on our journey, we have come a long way.
10. The team's success is a result of joint efforts.
11. I have learned a lot from this experience.
12. Let's look forward to achieving more in the future.
13. Your progress this year is outstanding.
14. We faced challenges but kept moving forward.
15. Celebrating progress is as important as making it.
16. This is a big step towards our future goals.
17. Your efforts are truly appreciated by everyone.
18. Keep aiming high; your ambition will lead you to success.
19. Reviewing our achievements shows how far we've come.
20. We are on the right path to greater accomplishments.

Key
Of
Exercises

Chapter: 1

Hello, how are you?
مرحبًا، كيف حالك؟
Marhaban, kayfa halak?

Good morning! How are you today?
صباح الخير! كيف حالك اليوم؟
Sabah al-khayr! Kayfa halak alyawm?

I'm fine, thank you. How are you?
أنا بخير، شكرًا. كيف حالك؟
Ana bekhayr, shukran. Kayfa halak?

My name is Ali. What is your name?
اسمي علي. ما اسمك؟
Ismi Ali. Ma ismuk?

Nice to meet you.
تشرفت بلقائك.
Tasharraft biliqa'ik.

I'm from India. Where are you from?
أنا من الهند. من أين أنت؟
Ana min al-Hind. Min ayna anta?

I'm fine as well. Thank you.
أنا بخير أيضًا. شكرًا.
Ana bekhayr ayzan. Shukran.

I am from Egypt.
أنا من مصر.
Ana min Misr.

Where are you from?
من أين أنت؟
Min ayna anta?

My name is Sarah. Nice to meet you.
.اسمي سارة. تشرفت بلقائك
Ismi Sarah. Tasharraft biliqa'ik.

Good evening! How are you?
مساء الخير! كيف حالك؟
Masa' al-khayr! Kayfa halak?

I am from Morocco. Where are you from?
أنا من المغرب. من أين أنت؟
Ana min al-Maghrib. Min ayna anta?

I'm fine, praise be to God.
.أنا بخير، الحمد لله
Ana bekhayr, alhamdulillah.

What's your name?
ما اسمك؟
Ma ismuk?

Hello, I am Ahmad. Nice to meet you.
.مرحبًا، أنا أحمد. تشرفت بلقائك
Marhaban, ana Ahmad. Tasharraft biliqa'ik.

I'm from Saudi Arabia. And you?
أنا من السعودية. وأنت؟
Ana min as-Su'udiyya. Wa anta?

Hello! My name is Youssef. How are you?
مرحبًا! اسمي يوسف. كيف حالك؟
Marhaban! Ismi Youssef. Kayfa halak?

I'm fine, thank you. What about you?
أنا بخير، شكرًا. وماذا عنك؟
Ana bekhayr, shukran. Wa madha ank?

Where are you from? I'm from Lebanon.
.من أين أنت؟ أنا من لبنان
Min ayna anta? Ana min Lubnan.

Nice to meet you too!
!تشرفت بلقائك أيضًا
Tasharraft biliqa'ik ayzan!

Chapter: 2

What is your nationality?
ما هي جنسيتك؟
Ma hiya jinsiyatak?

I am from India. Where are you from?
أنا من الهند. من أين أنت؟
Ana min al-Hind. Min ayna anta?

I am French. And you?
أنا فرنسي. وأنت؟
Ana Faransi. Wa anta?

Are you Egyptian?
هل أنت مصري؟
Hal anta Misri?

Yes, I am Egyptian.
.نعم، أنا مصري
Na'am, ana Misri.

He is from Saudi Arabia.
.هو من السعودية
Huwa min as-Su'udiyya.

She is American.
.هي أمريكية
Hiya Amrikiyya.

Where are you from?
من أين أنت؟
Min ayna anta?

I am from Morocco.
أنا من المغرب.
Ana min al-Maghrib.

My friend is British.
صديقي بريطاني.
Sadiqi Britani.

Is she from France?
هل هي من فرنسا؟
Hal hiya min Faransa?

He is not American.
هو ليس أمريكيًا.
Huwa laysa Amrikiyan.

My nationality is Indian.
جنسيتي هندية.
Jinsiyati Hindiyya.

What nationality are you?
ما هي جنسيتك؟
Ma hiya jinsiyatak?

I am from Saudi Arabia.
أنا من السعودية.
Ana min as-Su'udiyya.

Are you from Morocco?
هل أنت من المغرب؟
Hal anta min al-Maghrib?

She is not French.
هي ليست فرنسية.
Hiya laysa Faransiyya.

We are from Egypt.
نحن من مصر.
Nahnu min Misr.

I am not from America.
أنا لست من أمريكا.
Ana lastu min Amrika.

He is Saudi, but I am British.
هو سعودي، لكنني بريطاني.
Huwa Su'udi, lakinani Britani.

Chapter: 3

My family is large.
عائلتي كبيرة.
A'ilati kabira.

I have a father and a mother.
لدي أب وأم.
Laday ab wa um.

My brother is a student.
أخي طالب.
Akhi talib.

My sister is a teacher.
أختي معلمة.
Ukhti mu'allima.

We live together as a family.
نعيش معًا كعائلة.
Na'ish ma'an ka'a'ilah.

My grandfather is very wise.
جدي حكيم جدًا.
Jaddi hakim jiddan.

My grandmother loves to cook.
جدتي تحب الطهي.
Jaddati tuhibbu at-tahi.

I have one brother and one sister.
لدي أخ واحد وأخت واحدة.
Laday akh wahid wa ukht wahida.

My aunt is visiting us this week.
عمة زارتنا هذا الأسبوع.
Amma zaratna hadha al-usbu'a.

My uncle works in a bank.
عمي يعمل في بنك.
Ammi ya'mal fi bank.

My cousin is younger than me.
ابن عمي أصغر مني.
Ibn 'ammi asghar minni.

We are a close family.
نحن عائلة قريبة.
Nahnu 'a'ilah qariba.

How many members are in your family?
كم عدد الأعضاء في عائلتك؟
Kam 'adad al-a'ada fi 'a'ilatik?

I love my family very much.
أحب عائلتي كثيرًا.
Uhibbu 'a'ilati kathiran.

My parents support me in my studies.
والدي يدعمانني في دراستي.
Waliday yad'amanuni fi dirasati.

My brother plays football every weekend.
أخي يلعب كرة القدم كل عطلة نهاية الأسبوع.
Akhi yal'ab kurat al-qadam kul 'utlat nihayat al-usbu'a.

My sister enjoys painting.
أختي تستمتع بالرسم.
Ukhti tastamti'u bil-rasm.

My father has a good job.
أبي لديه وظيفة جيدة.
Abi ladayh wadhifa jayyida.

My mother takes care of the house.
أمي تهتم بالمنزل.
Ummii tahtam bil-manzil.

I often spend time with my cousins.
غالبًا ما أقضي وقتًا مع أبناء عمومتي.
Ghaliban ma aqdi waqtan ma'a abna' 'umumati.

Chapter: 4

I am an engineer.
أنا مهندس.
Ana muhandis.

My brother works as a lawyer.
أخي يعمل محاميًا.
Akhi ya'mal muhamiya.

She is a nurse at a hospital.
هي ممرضة في مستشفى.
Hiya mumarida fi mustashfa.

What does your father do for a living?
ماذا يعمل والدك لكسب العيش؟
Mada ya'mal waliduk likasb al-'aysh?

My mother works in a school.
والدتي تعمل في مدرسة.
Walidati ta'mal fi madrasah.

I work at a big company.
أعمل في شركة كبيرة.
A'mal fi sharika kabira.

He is a driver.
هو سائق.
Huwa sa'iq.

She is a cook at a restaurant.
هي طاهية في مطعم.
Hiya tahiya fi mat'am.

I have a friend who is a police officer.
لدي صديق يعمل ضابط شرطة.
Laday sadiq ya'mal dhabit shurta.

My uncle is a teacher.
عمي معلم.
Ammi mu'allim.

I work as a programmer.
أعمل مبرمجًا.
A'mal mubarmijaan.

Do you work with other people?
هل تعمل مع أشخاص آخرين؟
Hal ta'mal ma'a ashkhas akharin?

My cousin is a doctor.
ابن عمي طبيب.
Ibn 'ammi tabib.

Where do you work?
أين تعمل؟
Ayna ta'mal?

I work with a team of engineers.
أعمل مع فريق من المهندسين.
A'mal ma'a fareeq min al-muhandisin.

Our manager is very experienced.
مديرنا ذو خبرة كبيرة.
Mudiruna dhu khibra kabira.

I am a worker at a construction site.
أنا عامل في موقع بناء.
Ana 'amil fi mawaqi' bina'a.

He works in a hospital as a doctor.
يعمل في مستشفى كطبيب.
Ya'mal fi mustashfa katabib.

My sister is a lawyer.
أختي محامية.
Ukhti muhamiya.

Do you work at a company or a hospital?
هل تعمل في شركة أم مستشفى؟
Hal ta'mal fi sharika am mustashfa?

Chapter: 5

I wake up at 6 in the morning.
أستيقظ في السادسة صباحًا.
Astayqidh fi assadisah sabahan.

I go to work after breakfast.
أذهب إلى العمل بعد الإفطار.
Adhhab ila al'amal ba'd al-if'tar.

In the afternoon, I study at the university.
في فترة الظهيرة، أدرس في الجامعة.
Fi fatrat al-dhahira, adrus fi al-jamia.

I read a book in the evening.
أقرأ كتابًا في المساء.
Aqra'u kitabaan fi al-masaa.

I go to sleep at 9 o'clock.
أذهب إلى النوم في الساعة التاسعة.
Adhhab ila al-nawm fi al-saa'a al-tasi'a.

What do you do in the morning?
ماذا تفعل في الصباح؟
Mada taf'al fi al-sabah?

I eat lunch at 2 o’clock.
أتناول الغداء في الساعة الثانية.
Atanaawal al-ghadaa fi al-saa'a al-thaniyya.

I exercise every day.
أمارس الرياضة كل يوم.
Umaarisu al-riyadah kull yawm.

I work in the evening.
أعمل في المساء.
A'mal fi al-masaa.

I go to school in the morning.
أذهب إلى المدرسة في الصباح.
Adhhab ila al-madrasa fi al-sabah.

I return home after work.
أعود إلى المنزل بعد العمل.
A'ud ila al-manzil ba'd al-'amal.

I watch TV before dinner.
أشاهد التلفاز قبل العشاء.
Ushaahid al-tilfaz qabl al-'asha.

I have breakfast with my family.
أتناول الإفطار مع عائلتي.
Atanaawal al-if'tar ma'a 'ailati.

I study Arabic at night.
أدرس العربية في الليل.
Adrusu al-'arabiyya fi al-layl.

I cook dinner every day.
أطبخ العشاء كل يوم.
Atbukh al-'asha kull yawm.

I go out with friends on the weekend.
أخرج مع الأصدقاء في عطلة نهاية الأسبوع.
Akhruj ma'a al-asdiqa' fi 'utlat nihayat al-usbu'.

I wash my clothes in the evening.
أغسل ملابسي في المساء.
Aghsil malabisi fi al-masaa.

I have dinner at 7 o'clock.
أتناول العشاء في الساعة السابعة.
Atanaawal al-'asha fi al-saa'a al-sabi'a.

What time do you go to bed?
في أي وقت تذهب إلى السرير؟
Fi ay waqt tadhhab ila al-sareer?

I leave the house at 8 in the morning.
أخرج من المنزل في الساعة الثامنة صباحًا.
Akhruj min al-manzil fi al-saa'a al-thaminah sabahan.

Chapter: 6

I am hungry, I want to eat now.
أنا جائع، أريد أن آكل الآن.
Ana jaa'i'un, uridu an akul al-aan.

Do you have a table for four people?
هل لديك طاولة لأربعة أشخاص؟
Hal ladayka tawila li-arba'a ashkhas?

I want fish with rice, please.
أريد سمكًا مع الأرز، من فضلك.
Uridu samakan ma'a al-aruzz, min fadlak.

How much is the salad?
كم سعر السلطة؟
Kam si'r al-salata?

I want the drink without sugar.
أريد الشراب بدون سكر.
Uridu al-sharab bidun sukkar.

This dish is delicious.
هذا الطبق لذيذ.
Hatha al-tabaq latheeth.

Can I have water, please?
هل يمكنني الحصول على ماء، من فضلك؟
Hal yumkinuni al-husool 'ala ma', min fadlak?

I eat bread with my meal.
أتناول الخبز مع وجبتي.
Atanaawal al-khubz ma'a wajbati.

I want coffee in the morning.
أريد قهوة في الصباح.
Uridu qahwa fi al-sabah.

I don't want meat, I want vegetables.
لا أريد لحمًا، أريد خضروات.
La uridu lahman, uridu khudrawat.

Do you have dessert?
هل لديك حلوى؟
Hal ladayka halwa?

I would like a menu, please.
أود قائمة طعام، من فضلك.
Awad qaimat ta'am, min fadlak.

The bill, please.
الفاتورة، من فضلك.
Al-fatoora, min fadlak.

I am ready to order.
أنا مستعد للطلب.
Ana musta'id lil-talab.

What do you recommend?
ماذا تنصح؟
Mada tansah?

Do you have any chicken dishes?
هل لديك أطباق دجاج؟
Hal ladayka atbaq dajaj?

I want my food with a little salt.
أريد طعامي بقليل من الملح.
Uridu ta'ami bi-qaleel min al-mil'h.

Can I have tea?
هل يمكنني الحصول على شاي؟
Hal yumkinuni al-husool 'ala shay?

How much is the total?
كم هو الإجمالي؟
Kam huwa al-ijmaali?

Do you have vegetarian options?
هل لديك خيارات نباتية؟
Hal ladayka khayarat nabatiyya?

Chapter: 7

How much is the shirt?
كم سعر القميص؟
Kam si'r al-qamees?

I want a small size, please.
أريد مقاس صغير، من فضلك.
Uridu maqas sagheer, min fadlak.

This bag is expensive.
هذه الحقيبة غالية.
Hathihi al-haqeeba ghalia.

Can I get a discount?
هل يمكنني الحصول على خصم؟
Hal yumkinuni al-husool 'ala khasm?

I want to buy shoes.
أريد شراء حذاء.
Uridu shira' hidha'.

How much is this in cash?
كم يكلف هذا نقدًا؟
Kam yukalif hatha naqd-an?

Do you have red clothes?
هل لديك ملابس حمراء؟
Hal ladayka malabis hamra?

I will pay with a credit card.
سأدفع بواسطة بطاقة ائتمان.
Sa'adfa' biwasitat bitaqat i'timan.

I like green and blue colors.
أحب الألوان الخضراء والزرقاء.
Uhibb al-alwan al-khadra' wal-zarqa'.

This price is too high.
هذا السعر مرتفع جدًا.
Hatha al-si'r murtafa' jiddan.

I want to buy vegetables.
أريد شراء الخضروات.
Uridu shira' al-khudrawat.

Is this possible with a discount?
هل هذا ممكن مع خصم؟
Hal hatha mumkin ma'a khasm?

The market is busy today.
السوق مشغول اليوم.
Al-suq mashghool al-yawm.

Do you have white shoes?
هل لديك أحذية بيضاء؟
Hal ladayka ahdhiya bayda'?

The total is thirty dollars.
الإجمالي هو ثلاثون دولارًا.
Al-ijmaali huwa thalathun dollar-an.

I need to buy a gift.
أحتاج إلى شراء هدية.
Ahtaj ila shira' hadiya.

I am looking for a black shirt.
أبحث عن قميص أسود.
Abhath 'an qamees aswad.

This price is cheap.
هذا السعر رخيص.
Hatha al-si'r rakhis.

I like shopping at the market.
أحب التسوق في السوق.
Uhibb al-tasawwuq fi al-suq.

I want to buy this, how much is it?
أريد شراء هذا، كم سعره؟
Uridu shira' hatha, kam si'ruh?

Chapter: 8

My sister is beautiful and kind.
أختي جميلة ولطيفة.
Ukhti jameela wa lateefa.

He is tall but weak.
هو طويل ولكنه ضعيف.
Huwa taweel walakinahu da'eef.

She has blue eyes and blonde hair.
لديها عيون زرقاء وشعر أشقر.
Ladayha 'uyoon zarqa' wa sha'ar ashqar.

My father is calm and serious.
أبي هادئ وجاد.
Abi hadii wa jad.

I am a little nervous today.
أنا متوتر قليلاً اليوم.
Ana mutawattir qaleelan al-yawm.

You are generous and elegant.
أنت كريم وأنيق.
Anta kareem wa aneeq.

He is strong and smart.
هو قوي وذكي.
Huwa qawi wa dhaki.

I like patient people.
أحب الناس الصبورين.
Uhibb al-nas al-sabireen.

She looks beautiful in red.
تبدو جميلة باللون الأحمر.
Tabdu jameela bil-lawn al-ahmar.

He is quick-tempered sometimes.
هو سريع الغضب أحيانًا.
Huwa saree' al-ghadab ahyanan.

My friend is kind and helpful.
صديقي لطيف ومساعد.
Sadiqi lateef wa musaid.

She is fun and always smiling.
هي ممتعة ودائمًا مبتسمة.
Hiya mumti'a wa da'iman mubtasima.

He has a serious personality.
.لديه شخصية جدية
Ladayhi shakhsiyya jiddiya.

My mother is thin and kind.
.أمي نحيفة ولطيفة
Ummi naheefa wa lateefa.

You are very smart.
.أنت ذكي جدًا
Anta dhaki jiddan.

She is short and has green eyes.
.هي قصيرة ولديها عيون خضراء
Hiya qaseera wa ladayha 'uyoon khadra'.

My brother is strong but calm.
.أخي قوي ولكنه هادئ
Akhi qawi walakinahu hadii.

She is a little bit shy but kind.
.هي خجولة قليلاً ولكنها لطيفة
Hiya khajoola qaleelan walakinaha lateefa.

I am happy with my friend.
.أنا سعيد مع صديقي
Ana sa'eed ma'a sadiqi.

He is generous and always smiling.
.هو كريم ودائمًا مبتسم
Huwa kareem wa da'iman mubtasim.

Chapter: 9

I love reading books in my free time.
.أحب قراءة الكتب في وقت فراغي
Uhibbu qira'at al-kutub fi waqt faraghi.

He likes drawing and painting.
يحب الرسم والتلوين.
Yuhibbu al-rasm wa al-taleen.

She loves to cook new dishes.
تحب طهي الأطباق الجديدة.
Tuhibbu tahyi al-atbaaq al-jadida.

We go swimming on weekends.
نذهب للسباحة في عطلة نهاية الأسبوع.
Nadhhab lil-sibaha fi 'utlat nihayat al-usbu'.

They enjoy playing football.
يستمتعون بلعب كرة القدم.
Yastamti'oon bil'ib kurat al-qadam.

I watch TV every evening.
أشاهد التلفاز كل مساء.
Ushaahid al-tilfaz kull masa'.

She listens to music every day.
تستمع إلى الموسيقى كل يوم.
Tastami'u ila al-musiqa kull yawm.

He likes cycling with his friends.
يحب ركوب الدراجة مع أصدقائه.
Yuhibbu rukub al-darajah ma'a asdiqaa'ih.

My favourite hobby is traveling.
هوايتي المفضلة هي السفر.
Hawayati al-mufaddalah hiya al-safar.

I take photos of nature.
ألتقط صورًا للطبيعة.
Altiqat suran lil-tabee'a.

She enjoys dancing.
تستمتع بالرقص.
Tastamti'u bil-raqs.

He goes running in the morning.
يذهب للجري في الصباح.
Yadhhab lil-jari fi al-sabah.

I play football with my brother.
ألعب كرة القدم مع أخي.
Al'ab kurat al-qadam ma'a akhi.

We go shopping on Fridays.
نذهب للتسوق يوم الجمعة.
Nadhhab lil-tasawwuq yawma al-jum'a.

He likes to sing in his free time.
يحب الغناء في وقت فراغه.
Yuhibbu al-ghina' fi waqt faraghi.

I enjoy writing stories.
أستمتع بكتابة القصص.
Asta'mti'u bi-kitabati al-qisas.

She is good at photography.
هي جيدة في التصوير الفوتوغرافي.
Hiya jayyidah fi al-tasweer al-fotughrafi.

We love going out with friends.
نحب الخروج مع الأصدقاء.
Nuhibbu al-khuruj ma'a al-asdiqa.'

He likes sports and running.
يحب الرياضة والجري.
Yuhibbu al-riyada wa al-jari.

She spends her free time drawing.
تقضي وقت فراغها في الرسم.
Taqdi waqt faraghiha fi al-rasm.

Chapter: 10

Where is the nearest market?
أين أقرب سوق؟
Ayn aqrab suuq?

Go straight and turn left.
اذهب مباشرة ثم انعطف يسارًا.
Izhab mubasharatan thumma in'atif yasaran.

The station is far from here.
المحطة بعيدة من هنا.
Al-mahattah ba'idah min huna.

The bank is next to the post office.
البنك بجوار مكتب البريد.
Al-bank bijuwar maktab al-barid.

Is the park behind the school?
هل الحديقة خلف المدرسة؟
Hal al-hadiqah khalf al-madrasa?

The hotel is on the right.
الفندق على اليمين.
Al-funduq 'ala al-yamin.

Where is the main road?
أين الطريق الرئيسي؟
Ayn al-tariq al-ra'isi?

Turn left at the intersection.
انعطف يسارًا عند التقاطع.
In'atif yasaran 'inda al-taqatu.

The bus station is near the square.
محطة الحافلات قريبة من الساحة.
Mahattat al-hafalat qareebah min al-saha.

Go straight; the museum is on your left.
اذهب مباشرة؛ المتحف على يسارك.
Izhab mubasharatan; al-mat'haf 'ala yasarak.

Is it close to the city center?
هل هو قريب من وسط المدينة؟
Hal huwa qareeb min wasat al-madina?

The hospital is far, about ten minutes by car.
المستشفى بعيد، حوالي عشر دقائق بالسيارة.
Al-mustashfa ba'id, hawali 'ashr daqayeq bil-sayyara.

Go straight, then turn right at the traffic light.
اذهب مباشرة، ثم انعطف يمينًا عند إشارة المرور.
Izhab mubasharatan, thumma in'atif yaminan 'inda ishara al-murur.

The library is behind the big building.
المكتبة خلف المبنى الكبير.
Al-maktabah khalf al-mabna al-kabir.

The supermarket is next to the pharmacy.
السوبرماركت بجوار الصيدلية.
Al-supermarket bijuwar al-saydaliyah.

Can you tell me where the nearest bank is?
هل يمكنك أن تخبرني أين أقرب بنك؟
Hal yumkinuka an tukhbirni ayn aqrab bank?

The restaurant is in front of the train station.
المطعم أمام محطة القطار.
Al-mat'am amam mahattat al-qitar.

The mosque is on the left side of the street.
المسجد على الجانب الأيسر من الشارع.
Al-masjid 'ala al-janib al-ayser min al-shari'.

Is the café near the park?
هل المقهى قريب من الحديقة؟
Hal al-maqha qareeb min al-hadiqah?

The shopping mall is straight ahead, next to the hotel.
مركز التسوق أمامك مباشرة، بجوار الفندق.
Markaz al-tasawuq amamak mubasharatan, bijuwar al-funduq.

Chapter: 11

Where is the departure gate?
أين بوابة المغادرة؟
Ayn bawabat al-mughadara?

I need to check my luggage.
أحتاج إلى فحص أمتعتي.
Ahtaj ila fahs am'ti'ati.

The flight is delayed by one hour.
الرحلة متأخرة بساعة واحدة.
Al-rihlah muta'akhira bisaa'ah wahidah.

The customs office is on the right.
مكتب الجمارك على اليمين.
Maktab al-jamarik 'ala al-yamin.

Show your passport and boarding pass.
أظهر جواز سفرك وبطاقة الصعود.
Azhir jawaz safarak wa biṭaqat al-suud.

The airport is very busy today.
المطار مشغول جداً اليوم.
Al-maṭar mashghul jiddan al-yawm.

Where is the check-in counter?
أين مكتب تسجيل الوصول؟
Ayn maktab tajil al-wusul?

My bag is too heavy; can I remove some items?
حقيبتي ثقيلة جداً؛ هل يمكنني إزالة بعض الأغراض؟
Haqqibati thaqila jiddan; hal yumkinuni izalat ba'd al-aghrad?

I am traveling on an international flight.
أنا أسافر على رحلة دولية.
Ana usafir 'ala riḥlah dawliyah.

Where can I find the information desk?
أين يمكنني العثور على مكتب المعلومات؟
Ayn yumkinuni al-'uthur 'ala maktab al-ma'lumat?

The arrival hall is on the second floor.
قاعة الوصول في الطابق الثاني.
Qā'at al-wusul fi al-ṭābiq al-thani.

Is the visa required for this flight?
هل الفيزا مطلوبة لهذه الرحلة؟
Hal al-fiza maṭlūbah lihādhihi al-riḥlah?

I need to confirm my booking.
أحتاج إلى تأكيد حجزي.
Ahtaj ila ta'kid ḥajzi.

The plane will board at gate 7.
ستبدأ عملية الصعود على البوابة 7.
Satabda 'amaliyat al-suud 'ala al-bawabah 7.

How many bags can I carry?
كم عدد الحقائب التي يمكنني حملها؟
Kam 'adad al-ḥaqa'ib allati yumkinuni hamluha?

The flight is at 9 in the morning.
الرحلة في الساعة 9 صباحًا.
Al-rihlah fi al-sa'ah 9 sabahan.

Where is the security checkpoint?
أين نقطة التفتيش الأمنية؟
Ayn nuqtat al-taftish al-amniyah?

I need help finding my boarding gate.
أحتاج إلى مساعدة في العثور على بوابة الصعود.
Ahtaj ila musā'adah fi al-'uthur 'ala bawabat al-suud.

Is there a delay in the departure?
هل هناك تأخير في المغادرة؟
Hal hunak ta'khīr fi al-mughādrah?

Can I change my seat at the counter?
هل يمكنني تغيير مقعدي عند المكتب؟
Hal yumkinuni taghyir maq'adi 'inda al-maktab?

Chapter: 12

I have a headache and a fever.
لدي صداع وحمى.
Ladi ṣudā' wa ḥummā.

Can I book an appointment with the doctor today?
هل يمكنني حجز موعد مع الطبيب اليوم؟
Hal yumkinuni ḥajz mawa'id ma'a al-ṭabīb al-yawm?

The doctor said I need to rest.
قال الطبيب إنني بحاجة إلى الراحة.
Qāla al-ṭabīb innani biḥājah ila al-rāḥah.

I need to take the medicine three times a day.
أحتاج إلى تناول الدواء ثلاث مرات في اليوم.
Ahtāj ila tanāwul al-dawā' thalāth marrāt fi al-yawm.

Where is the emergency room in the hospital?
أين غرفة الطوارئ في المستشفى؟
Ayn ghuftat al-ṭawāri' fi al-mustashfā?

I feel dizzy and tired.
أشعر بالدوار والتعب.
Aš'ūr bil-dawār wa al-ta'ab.

My child has a high fever and a cough.
طفلي لديه حمى عالية وسعال.
Tifli ladayh ḥummā 'āliyah wa su'āl.

The doctor is examining the patient now.
الطبيب يقوم بفحص المريض الآن.
Al-ṭabīb yaqūm bi-faḥṣ al-marīḍ al-ān.

What is your blood pressure reading?
ما قراءة ضغط دمك؟
Mā qirā'at ḍaght damak?

I have an appointment at the clinic at 10 o'clock.
لدي موعد في العيادة الساعة 10.
Ladi mawa'id fi al-'iyādah al-sā'ah 10.

I need medicine for a stomach ache.
أحتاج إلى دواء لآلام المعدة.
Ahtāj ila dawā' li-ālam al-ma'ida.

How long have you been feeling this pain?
منذ متى وأنت تشعر بهذا الألم؟
Mundhu matā wa anta taš'ūr bihādhā al-alam?

I will go to the hospital if my condition worsens.
سأذهب إلى المستشفى إذا ساءت حالتي.
Sa'adhhab ila al-mustashfā idhā sā'at ḥālati.

Is there any pharmacy nearby?
هل هناك أي صيدلية قريبة؟
Hal hunāk ay ṣaydaliyah qarībah?

I need an injection for the pain.
أحتاج إلى حقنة للألم.
Ahtāj ila ḥuqnah lil-alam.

The doctor gave me a prescription for antibiotics.
أعطاني الطبيب وصفة للمضادات الحيوية.
A'ṭānī al-ṭabīb waṣfah lil-muḍādāt al-ḥayawiyyah.

I am feeling better after taking the medicine.
أشعر بتحسن بعد تناول الدواء.
Aš'ūr bi-taḥassun ba'd tanāwul al-dawā'

The nurse will check your temperature.
الممرضة ستقوم بفحص حرارتك.
Al-mumariḍah sataqūm bi-faḥṣ ḥarārātak.

Do you have any allergies to medicine?
هل لديك أي حساسية من الأدوية؟
Hal ladayk ay ḥasāsiyyah min al-adwiyah?

I have a pain in my chest; I need to see a doctor urgently.
أشعر بألم في صدري؛ أحتاج إلى رؤية طبيب على وجه السرعة.
Aš'ūr bi-alam fī ṣadrī; aḥtāj ila ru'yat ṭabīb 'ala wajh al-sur'ah.

Chapter: 13

Today's weather is sunny and beautiful.
طقس اليوم مشمس وجميل.
Ṭaqs al-yawm mushmis wa jamīl.

The temperature is cold in winter.
درجة الحرارة باردة في الشتاء.
Darajat al-ḥarārah bāridah fī al-shitā'.

I love the spring season because of the flowers.
أحب فصل الربيع بسبب الزهور.
Uḥibb faṣl al-rabī' bisabab al-zuhūr.

How is the weather in your city today?
كيف الطقس في مدينتك اليوم؟
Kayfa al-ṭaqs fī madīnatak al-yawm?

It's raining, and the sky is cloudy.
إنها تمطر، والسماء غائمة.
Innahā tumṭir, wa al-samā' ghā'imah.

Summer is hot and dry in my country.
الصيف حار وجاف في بلدي.
Al-ṣayf ḥār wa jāf fi baladī.

I prefer autumn because it's cool and windy.
أفضل فصل الخريف لأنه بارد وعاصف.
Ufaḍḍil faṣl al-kharīf li-annahu bārid wa 'āṣif.

The weather forecast says it will snow tomorrow.
تقول توقعات الطقس إنه سيتساقط الثلج غدًا.
Taqūl tawq'āt al-ṭaqs innahu sayatasaqṭ al-thalj ghadan.

We need to wear warm clothes in winter.
نحتاج إلى ارتداء ملابس دافئة في الشتاء.
Naḥtāj ila irtida' malābis dāfi'ah fi al-shitā'.

I don't like humid weather; it's uncomfortable.
لا أحب الطقس الرطب؛ إنه غير مريح.
Lā uḥibb al-ṭaqs al-raṭb; innahu ghayr murīḥ.

The sun sets at seven in the evening.
تغرب الشمس في السابعة مساءً.
Taghrub al-shams fi al-sābi'ah masā'an.

There is a storm coming this evening.
هناك عاصفة قادمة هذا المساء.
Hunāk 'āṣifah qādimah hādhā al-masā'.

The weather is windy today; let's stay indoors.
الطقس عاصف اليوم؛ دعنا نبقى في الداخل.
Al-ṭaqs 'āṣif al-yawm; da'nā nabqā fi al-dākhil.

It's a good day for a walk because it's cool and sunny.
إنه يوم جيد للتنزه لأنه بارد ومشمس.
Innahu yawm jayyid lil-tanazzuh li-annahu bārid wa mushmis.

Is it raining now, or is it still dry?
هل تمطر الآن، أم لا تزال جافة؟
Hal tumṭir al-ān, am lā tāzil jāfah?

The sky is clear, and there are no clouds.
السماء صافية، ولا توجد سُحب.
Al-samā' ṣāfiyah, wa lā tūjad suḥub.

In autumn, the leaves fall from the trees.
في الخريف، تسقط الأوراق من الأشجار.
Fi al-kharīf, tasqiṭ al-awrāq min al-ashjār.

What is the temperature today?
ما درجة الحرارة اليوم؟
Mā darajat al-ḥarārah al-yawm?

Summer is my favorite season because I love the sun.
الصيف هو فصلي المفضل لأنني أحب الشمس.
Al-ṣayf huwa faṣlī al-mufaḍḍal li-annani uḥibb al-shams.

I heard it will be a rainy day tomorrow.
سمعت أنه سيكون يومًا ممطرًا غدًا.
Sami't annahu sayakūn yawman mumṭiran ghadan.

Chapter: 14

What time is the meeting today?
في أي وقت الاجتماع اليوم؟
Fī ayy waqt al-ijtimā' al-yawm?

The date today is the 15th of March.
تاريخ اليوم هو الخامس عشر من مارس.
Tārīkh al-yawm huwa al-khāmis 'ashar min Mārīs.

I wake up at seven in the morning.
أستيقظ في السابعة صباحًا.
Astaqẖiẓ fī al-sābi'ah ṣabāḥan.

My birthday is next week.
عيد ميلادي الأسبوع المقبل.
'Īd mīlādī al-usbū' al-muqbil.

We have a meeting at two o'clock in the afternoon.
لدينا اجتماع في الثانية بعد الظهر.
Ladaynā ijtimā' fī al-thāniyah ba'd al-ẓuhr.

What day is it today?
أي يوم هو اليوم؟
Ayy yawm huwa al-yawm?

I am busy now; can we meet later?
أنا مشغول الآن؛ هل يمكننا الالتقاء لاحقًا؟
Anā mashghūl al-ān; hal yumkinunā al-iltikā' lāḥiqan?

The flight is on Friday at noon.
الرحلة يوم الجمعة في الظهر.
Al-riḥlah yawm al-jum'ah fī al-ẓuhr.

I am free on Sunday; let's meet then.
أنا متفرغ يوم الأحد؛ دعنا نلتقي حينها.
Anā mutafarriġ yawm al-Aḥad; da'nā naltiqī ḥīnahā.

The class starts at ten and ends at eleven.
تبدأ الحصة في الساعة العاشرة وتنتهي في الساعة الحادية عشرة.
Tabda' al-ḥiṣṣah fī al-sā'ah al-'āshirah wa tantahī fī al-sā'ah al-ḥādiyah 'ashrah.

What is the time difference between our countries?
ما هو فرق التوقيت بين بلدينا؟
Mā huwa farq al-tawqīt bayna baladaynā?

I will call you at eight in the evening.
سأتصل بك في الثامنة مساءً.
Sa'attāṣil bik fī al-thāminah masā'an.

Yesterday was a busy day at work.
كان يوم أمس يومًا مشغولًا في العمل.
Kān yawm ams yawman mashghūlan fī al-'amal.

Let’s meet at the restaurant at six.
دعنا نلتقي في المطعم في الساعة السادسة.
Da'nā naltiqī fī al-maṭ‘am fī al-sā'ah al-sādisah.

The weekend starts on Thursday evening.
يبدأ عطلة نهاية الأسبوع مساء يوم الخميس.
Yabda' 'uṭlat nihāyat al-usbū' masā'an yawm al-khamīs.

How many hours are in a day?
كم عدد الساعات في اليوم؟
Kam 'adad al-sā'āt fī al-yawm?

We need to leave before the evening.
نحتاج إلى المغادرة قبل المساء.
Naḥtāj ilā al-mughādrah qabla al-masā'.

The event will take place next month.
سيحدث الحدث الشهر المقبل.
Sayuḥduth al-ḥadath al-shahr al-muqbil.

What time will you arrive?
في أي وقت ستصل؟
Fī ayy waqt sataṣil?

I will be ready in five minutes.
سأكون جاهزًا في خمس دقائق.
Sa'ākūn jāhizān fī khams daqā'iq.

Chapter: 15

I prefer tea over coffee.
أفضّل الشاي على القهوة.
Ufaḍḍil al-shāy 'alā al-qahwa.

In my opinion, this book is good.
في رأيي، هذا الكتاب جيد.
Fī ra'yī, hādhā al-kitāb jayyid.

I like movies, especially action movies.
أحب الأفلام، خاصة أفلام الأكشن.
Uḥibb al-aflām, khāṣṣatan aflāmm al-action.

I think this shirt is better than that one.
أعتقد أن هذه القميص أفضل من ذلك.
A'taqid anna hādhā al-qamīṣ afḍal min dhālik.

I don't like spicy food.
لا أحب الطعام الحار.
Lā uḥibb al-ṭa'ām al-ḥār.

He prefers reading to watching TV.
هو يفضّل القراءة على مشاهدة التلفاز.
Huwa yufaḍḍil al-qirā'ah 'alā mushāhadat al-tilfāz.

This restaurant is good, but I think it's too expensive.
هذا المطعم جيد، لكن أعتقد أنه مكلف جدًا.
Hādhā al-maṭ'am jayyid, lākin a'taqid annahu mukallif jiddan.

I agree; the service here is excellent.
أوافق؛ الخدمة هنا ممتازة.
Awāfiq; al-khidmah hunā mumtāzah.

I hate waiting in long lines.
أكره الانتظار في الطوابير الطويلة.
Akrh al-intiẓār fī al-ṭawābīr al-ṭawīlah.

What is your opinion about this movie?
ما رأيك في هذا الفيلم؟
Mā ra'yuk fī hādhā al-film?

I think the design is perfect.
أعتقد أن التصميم مثالي.
A'taqid anna al-taṣmīm mithālī.

Do you agree with my opinion?
هل توافق على رأيي؟
Hal tūāfiq 'alā ra'yī?

I would like to try a different flavor.
أود أن أجرب نكهة مختلفة.
Awad an ajarrib nakhah mukhtalifah.

I believe this brand is the best.
أعتقد أن هذه العلامة التجارية هي الأفضل.
A'taqid anna hādhih al-‘alāmah al-tijāriyah hiya al-afḍal.

I like summer, but I prefer winter.
أحب الصيف، لكن أفضّل الشتاء.
Uḥibb al-ṣayf, lākin ufaḍḍil al-shitā'.

He doesn’t like cold weather.
هو لا يحب الطقس البارد.
Huwa lā yuḥibb al-ṭaqs al-bārid.

I think it’s important to listen to everyone’s opinion.
أعتقد أنه من المهم الاستماع إلى آراء الجميع.
A'taqid annahu min al-muhimm al-istimā' ilā āra' al-jamīʿ.

She prefers working alone.
هي تفضّل العمل بمفردها.
Hī tafḍil al-‘amal bimufriḍihā.

I like the idea; it’s very creative.
أحب الفكرة؛ إنها مبتكرة جدًا.
Uḥibb al-fikrah; innahā mubtakirah jiddan.

In my opinion, the quality could be better.
في رأيي، الجودة يمكن أن تكون أفضل.
Fī ra'yī, al-jawdah yumkin an takūn afḍal.

Chapter: 16

The market is far from the office.
السوق بعيد عن المكتب.
Al-sūq bāʿid ʿan al-maktab.

Go left, then turn right at the street.
اذهب يسارًا، ثم انعطف يمينًا عند الشارع.
Ithhab yasāran, thumma inʿaṭif yamīnan ʿinda al-shāriʿ.

The library is behind the school.
المكتبة خلف المدرسة.
Al-maktabah khalf al-madrasa.

The hotel is in front of the restaurant.
الفندق أمام المطعم.
Al-funduq amām al-maṭʿam.

Is the train station near the main road?
هل محطة القطار قريبة من الطريق الرئيسي؟
Hal maḥaṭṭat al-qiṭār qarībah min al-ṭarīq al-ra'īsī?

The office is in the center of the city.
المكتب في وسط المدينة.
Al-maktab fī waṣṭ al-madīnah.

The hospital is opposite the market.
المستشفى مقابل السوق.
Al-mustashfā muqābil al-sūq.

The restaurant is next to the hotel.
المطعم بجوار الفندق.
Al-maṭʿam bijiwār al-funduq.

Is there a pharmacy near here?
هل هناك صيدلية قريبة من هنا؟
Hal hunāk ṣaydaliyya qarībah min hunā?

The road to the park is straight ahead.
الطريق إلى الحديقة أمامك.
Al-ṭarīq ilā al-ḥadīqah amāmak.

The market is on the left side.
السوق على الجانب الأيسر.
Al-sūq ʿalā al-jānib al-ayser.

I need directions to the library.
أحتاج إلى إرشادات للمكتبة.
Aḥtāj ilā irshādāt lil-maktabah.

The school is in the middle of the city.
المدرسة في وسط المدينة.
Al-madrasa fī waṣṭ al-madīnah.

The hotel is on the main street.
الفندق على الشارع الرئيسي.
Al-funduq ʿalā al-shāriʿ al-raʾīsī.

The bus station is near the library.
محطة الباص قريبة من المكتبة.
Maḥaṭṭat al-bāṣ qarībah min al-maktabah.

The coffee shop is next to the park.
المقهى بجوار الحديقة.
Al-maqha bijiwār al-ḥadīqah.

Where is the main square located?
أين تقع الساحة الرئيسية؟
Ayna taqaʿ al-sāḥah al-raʾīsīyah?

The bank is on the right side of the street.
البنك على الجانب الأيمن من الشارع.
Al-bank ʿalā al-jānib al-ayman min al-shāriʿ.

I prefer to take the main road to the hotel.
أفضّل أخذ الطريق الرئيسي إلى الفندق.
Ufaḍḍil akhḍ al-ṭarīq al-raʾīsī ilā al-funduq.

Is there a parking lot near the market?
هل هناك موقف سيارات قريب من السوق؟
Hal hunāk mawqif sayyārāt qarīb min al-sūq?

Chapter: 17

I have a meeting tomorrow.
لدي اجتماع غدًا.
Ladī ijtimāʿ ghadān.

Can we reschedule the appointment?
هل يمكننا إعادة جدولة الموعد؟
Hal yumkinunā iʿādat jadwalat al-mawʿid?

I want to confirm the reservation.
أريد تأكيد الحجز.
Urīdu taʾkīd al-ḥajz.

We have a plan to meet at 6 PM.
لدينا خطة للاجتماع الساعة 6 مساءً.
Ladaynā khuṭṭah lil-ijtimāʿ al-sāʿah 6 masāʾan.

Sorry, I need to cancel the dinner.
عذرًا، أحتاج إلى إلغاء العشاء.
ʿUḏran, aḥtāj ilā il-ghāʾ al-ʿashāʾ.

Do you want to make a new plan?
هل تريد وضع خطة جديدة؟
Hal turīd waḍʿ khuṭṭah jadīdah?

I am busy on Friday.
أنا مشغول يوم الجمعة.
Anā mashghūl yawm al-jumʿah.

Can you attend the meeting?
هل يمكنك حضور الاجتماع؟
Hal yumkinuka ḥuḍūr al-ijtimāʿ?

I hope to see you soon.
آمل أن أراك قريبًا.
Āmil an arāka qarīban.

Let's meet later.
لنلتقِ لاحقًا.
Linaltaqī lāḥiqan.

The reservation is for two people.
الحجز لشخصين.
Al-ḥajz li-shakhsayn.

What time suits you?
أي وقت يناسبك؟
Ay waqt yunāsibuka?

Shall we meet in the morning?
هل نلتقي في الصباح؟
Hal naltaqī fī al-ṣabāḥ?

I have an appointment at the office.
لدي موعد في المكتب.
Ladī maw'id fī al-maktab.

Can we make a plan for tomorrow?
هل يمكننا وضع خطة للغد؟
Hal yumkinunā waḍ' khuṭṭah lil-ghad?

I need to postpone the meeting.
أحتاج إلى تأجيل الاجتماع.
Aḥtāj ilā ta'jīl al-ijtimā'.

The new time is perfect.
الوقت الجديد ممتاز.
Al-waqt al-jadīd mumtāz.

Thank you for changing the plan.
شكرًا لتغيير الخطة.
Shukran litaghyīr al-khuṭṭah.

I am available on Saturday.
أنا متاح يوم السبت.
Anā mutāḥ yawm al-sabt.

Let's confirm the plan for next week.
دعنا نؤكد الخطة للأسبوع المقبل.
Daʿnā nuʾakkid al-khuṭṭah lil-usbūʿ al-muqbil.

Chapter: 18

Can you help me with this?
هل يمكنك مساعدتي في هذا؟
Hal yumkinuka musāʿadatī fī hādhā?

I need urgent help.
أحتاج إلى مساعدة عاجلة.
Aḥtāj ilā musāʿadah ʿājilah.

How can I offer help?
كيف يمكنني تقديم المساعدة؟
Kayfa yumkinunī taqdīm al-musāʿadah?

The ambulance is coming soon.
سيارة الإسعاف قادمة قريبًا.
Sayyārat al-ʾisʿāf qādimah qarīban.

Thank you for your assistance.
شكرًا لمساعدتك.
Shukran limusāʿadatika.

Do you need any help with this?
هل تحتاج إلى أي مساعدة في هذا؟
Hal taḥtāj ilā ay musāʿadah fī hādhā?

I am lost, can you guide me?
أنا ضائع، هل يمكنك إرشادي؟
Anā ḍāʾiʿ, hal yumkinuka irshādī?

He needs medical help immediately.
يحتاج إلى مساعدة طبية على الفور.
Yaḥtāj ilā musāʿadah ṭibbiyah ʿalā al-fawr.

Sorry, I cannot help right now.
عذرًا، لا أستطيع المساعدة الآن.
ʿUḏran, lā astaṭīʿ al-musāʿadah al-ān.

Can you call the police, please?
هل يمكنك الاتصال بالشرطة، من فضلك؟
Hal yumkinuka al-ittiṣāl bil-shurṭah, min faḍlik?

I am glad to assist you.
أنا سعيد بمساعدتك.
Anā saʿīd bimūsāʿadatika.

No problem, I will handle it.
لا مشكلة، سأتعامل مع ذلك.
Lā mushkilah, saʾataʿāmal maʿ dhālik.

Is there any danger here?
هل هناك أي خطر هنا؟
Hal hunāk ay khatar hunā?

I lost my way, can you help?
ضيعت طريقي، هل يمكنك المساعدة؟
Ḍayyaʿt ṭarīqī, hal yumkinuka al-musāʿadah?

What kind of help do you need?
ما نوع المساعدة التي تحتاجها؟
Mā nawʿ al-musāʿadah allatī taḥtājuhā?

Please wait, I will get help.
يرجى الانتظار، سأحضر المساعدة.
Yurjā al-intiẓār, saʾuḥḍir al-musāʿadah.

I will call for help right away.
سأطلب المساعدة على الفور.
Saʾaṭlub al-musāʿadah ʿalā al-fawr.

Are you in trouble? Do you need help?
هل أنت في مشكلة؟ هل تحتاج إلى مساعدة؟
Hal anta fī mushkilah? Hal taḥtāj ilā musāʿadah?

Help is on the way, stay calm.
المساعدة في الطريق، ابق هادئًا.
Al-musāʿadah fī al-ṭarīq, ibqā hādīʾan.

You are very kind, thank you.
أنت لطيف جدًا، شكرًا لك.
Anta laṭīf jiddan, shukran lak.

Chapter: 19

I use my phone every day.
أستخدم هاتفي كل يوم.
Ustaʿmidu hātifī kulla yawm.

Can you help me log into my account?
هل يمكنك مساعدتي في تسجيل الدخول إلى حسابي؟
Hal yumkinuka musāʿadatī fī tasjīl al-dukhūl ilā ḥisābī?

I like to post pictures on social media.
أحب نشر الصور على وسائل التواصل الاجتماعي.
Uḥibbu nashr al-ṣuwar ʿalā wasāʾil al-tawāṣul al-ijtimāʿī.

What is your favourite app?
ما هو تطبيقك المفضل؟
Mā huwa taṭbīquka al-mufaḍḍal?

The internet is very useful.
الإنترنت مفيد جدًا.
Al-internet mufīd jiddan.

I forgot my password, can you help?
نسيت كلمة المرور، هل يمكنك المساعدة؟
Nasītu kalimat al-murūr, hal yumkinuka al-musāʿadah?

I want to watch a video on YouTube.
أريد مشاهدة فيديو على يوتيوب.
Urīdu mushāhadat fīdyū ʿalā Yūtiūb.

Do you have an email account?
هل لديك حساب بريد إلكتروني؟
Hal ladayka ḥisāb barīd iliktrūnī?

Please share the picture with me.
يرجى مشاركة الصورة معي.
Yurjā mushārakat al-ṣūrah maʿī.

How can I download this app?
كيف يمكنني تحميل هذا التطبيق؟
Kayfa yumkinunī taḥmīl hādhā al-taṭbīq?

I enjoy watching live videos.
أستمتع بمشاهدة الفيديوهات المباشرة.
Astamtiʿ bimushāhadat al-fīdyūhāt al-mubāshirah.

Social media is very popular.
وسائل التواصل الاجتماعي شائعة جدًا.
Wasāʾil al-tawāṣul al-ijtimāʿī shāʾiʿah jiddan.

Can you send me a message on my phone?
هل يمكنك إرسال رسالة على هاتفي؟
Hal yumkinuka irsāl risālah ʿalā hātifī?

My device is not working, can you fix it?
جهازي لا يعمل، هل يمكنك إصلاحه؟
Jihāzī lā yaʿmal, hal yumkinuka iṣlāḥuhu?

I want to follow your account.
أريد متابعة حسابك.
Urīdu mutābaʿat ḥisābik.

He likes to comment on posts.
يحب التعليق على المنشورات.
Yuḥibbu al-taʿlīq ʿalā al-manshūrāt.

I need to update my app.
أحتاج إلى تحديث تطبيقي.
Aḥtāju ilā taḥdīth taṭbīqī.

She posted a video yesterday.
نشرت فيديو بالأمس.
Nasharat fīdyū bil-ʾams.

I prefer using my laptop for work.
أفضل استخدام حاسوبي المحمول للعمل.
Ufaddil istiʿmāl ḥāsūbī al-maḥmūl lil-ʿamal.

Technology makes life easier.
التكنولوجيا تجعل الحياة أسهل.
Al-tekhnūlūjiyā tajʿal al-ḥayāh ashal.

Chapter: 20

The table is round and made of wood.
الطاولة مستديرة ومصنوعة من الخشب.
Al-ṭāwilah mustadīrah wa-maṣnūʿah min al-khashab.

This box is small and light.
هذه العلبة صغيرة وخفيفة.
Hādhihi al-ʿulbah ṣaghīrah wa-khafīfah.

I have a beautiful red dress.
لدي فستان أحمر جميل.
Laday fustān aḥmar jamīl.

The metal chair is heavy but strong.
الكرسي المعدني ثقيل ولكنه قوي.
Al-kursī al-maʿdanī thaqīl walākinahu qawī.

My phone is new and made of plastic.
هاتفي جديد ومصنوع من البلاستيك.
Hātifī jadīd wa-maṣnūʿ min al-blāstīk.

The old sofa is comfortable and soft.
الأريكة القديمة مريحة وناعمة.
Al-arīkah al-qadīmah murīḥah wa-nāʿimah.

The blue cup is big and heavy.
الكوب الأزرق كبير وثقيل.
Al-kūb al-azraq kabīr wa-thaqīl.

The car is long and red.
السيارة طويلة وحمراء.
Al-sayyārah ṭawīlah wa-ḥamrā᾽.

This pen is small and made of metal.
هذا القلم صغير ومصنوع من المعدن.
Hādhā al-qalam ṣaghīr wa-maṣnū‘ min al-ma‘dan.

The bag is black and ugly.
الحقيبة سوداء وقبيحة.
Al-ḥaqībah sawdā᾽ wa-qabīḥah.

The book is big and has a blue cover.
الكتاب كبير وله غلاف أزرق.
Al-kitāb kabīr wa-lahu ghilāf azraq.

The box is light and square.
العلبة خفيفة ومربعة.
Al-‘ulbah khafīfah wa-murabba‘ah.

I like the yellow chair; it's comfortable.
أحب الكرسي الأصفر؛ إنه مريح.
Uḥibbu al-kursī al-aṣfar; innahu murīḥ.

The old phone is heavy and ugly.
الهاتف القديم ثقيل وقبيح.
Al-hātif al-qadīm thaqīl wa-qabīḥ.

This table is beautiful and round.
هذه الطاولة جميلة ومستديرة.
Hādhihi al-ṭāwilah jamīlah wa-mustadīrah.

The watch is small and made of metal.
الساعة صغيرة ومصنوعة من المعدن.
Al-sā‘ah ṣaghīrah wa-maṣnū‘ah min al-ma‘dan.

The picture is beautiful and colorful.
الصورة جميلة وملونة.
Al-ṣūrah jamīlah wa-mulawwanah.

I bought a new blue bag yesterday.
اشتريت حقيبة زرقاء جديدة أمس.
Ishtaraytu ḥaqībah zarqāʾ jadīdah ams.

This wooden chair is very comfortable.
هذا الكرسي الخشبي مريح جدًا.
Hādhā al-kursī al-khashabī murīḥ jiddan.

The plastic cup is light and green.
الكوب البلاستيكي خفيف وأخضر.
Al-kūb al-blāstīkī khafīf wa-akhaḍar.

Chapter: 21

I have a reservation for a single room.
لدي حجز لغرفة فردية.
Laday ḥajz li-ghurfah fardiyyah.

The hotel is clean and big.
الفندق نظيف وكبير.
Al-funduq naẓīf wa-kabīr.

Can I get a key for my room?
هل يمكنني الحصول على مفتاح غرفتي؟
Hal yumkinunī al-ḥuṣūl ʿalā miftāḥ ghurfatī?

I need room service for dinner.
أحتاج إلى خدمة الغرف للعشاء.
Aḥtāju ilā khidmat al-ghuraf lil-ʿashāʾ.

How much is the price per night?
كم سعر الليلة؟
Kam siʿr al-laylah?

Is there a restaurant in the hotel?
هل يوجد مطعم في الفندق؟
Hal yūjad maṭʿam fī al-funduq?

I would like to check out tomorrow.
أود تسجيل الخروج غدًا.
Awaddu tasjīl al-khurūj ghadan.

The laundry service is very helpful.
خدمة الغسيل مفيدة جدًا.
Khidmat al-ghasīl mufīdah jiddan.

The reception is on the first floor.
الاستقبال في الطابق الأول.
Al-istiqbāl fī al-ṭābiq al-awwal.

I want to make a call to my friend.
أريد إجراء مكالمة لصديقي.
Urīdu ijrāʾ mukālamah li-ṣadīqī.

Is the air conditioning working?
هل يعمل التكييف؟
Hal yaʿmal al-takyīf?

The buffet has many delicious dishes.
البوفيه يحتوي على العديد من الأطباق اللذيذة.
Al-būfīh yaḥtawī ʿalā al-ʿadīd min al-aṭbāq al-ladhīdhah.

My room is very comfortable and quiet.
غرفتي مريحة جدًا وهادئة.
Ghurfatī murīḥah jiddan wa-hādiʾah.

Can I request a late check-out?
هل يمكنني طلب تسجيل الخروج المتأخر؟
Hal yumkinunī ṭalab tasjīl al-khurūj al-mutaʾakhkhar?

The hotel is crowded during the holidays.
الفندق مزدحم خلال العطلات.
Al-funduq muzdaḥim khilāl al-ʿuṭalāt.

I need a taxi to the airport.
أحتاج إلى سيارة أجرة إلى المطار.
Aḥtāju ilā sayyārat ujrah ilā al-maṭār.

The breakfast is included in the price.
الإفطار مشمول في السعر.
Al-ifṭār mashmūl fī al-si‘r.

Is there free Wi-Fi in the hotel?
هل يوجد واي فاي مجاني في الفندق؟
Hal yūjad wāy fāy majjānī fī al-funduq?

I would like to change my room.
أود تغيير غرفتي.
Awaddu taghyīr ghurfatī.

Thank you for your excellent service.
شكرًا على خدمتك الممتازة.
Shukran ‘alā khidmatika al-mumtāzah.

Chapter: 22

The apartment is big and has two rooms.
الشقة كبيرة وتحتوي على غرفتين.
Al-shaqqah kabīrah wa taḥtawī ‘alā ghurfatayn.

How much is the rent for the house?
كم إيجار المنزل؟
Kam ījār al-manzil?

The contract is for one year.
العقد لمدة سنة واحدة.
Al-‘aqd limuddah sanah wāḥidah.

I would like to rent a furnished apartment.
أود استئجار شقة مفروشة.
Awaddu isti’jār shaqqah mafrooshah.

The kitchen is small but clean.
المطبخ صغير ولكنه نظيف.
Al-maṭbakh ṣaghīr walākinahu naẓīf.

Is the deposit refundable?
هل التأمين قابل للاسترداد؟
Hal al-taʾmīn qābil lil-istirdād?

The apartment is on the third floor.
الشقة في الطابق الثالث.
Al-shaqqah fī al-ṭābiq al-thālith.

I need a house with a large living room.
أحتاج إلى منزل بغرفة معيشة كبيرة.
Aḥtāju ilā manzil bi-ghurfat maʿīshah kabīrah.

Does the rent include water and electricity?
هل يشمل الإيجار الماء والكهرباء؟
Hal yashmal al-ījār al-māʾ wa al-kahrabāʾ?

I am looking for an unfurnished apartment.
أبحث عن شقة غير مفروشة.
Abḥath ʿan shaqqah ghayr mafrooshah.

The bathroom is modern and spacious.
الحمام حديث وواسع.
Al-ḥammām ḥadīth wa wāsiʿ.

Can I sign the lease agreement today?
هل يمكنني توقيع عقد الإيجار اليوم؟
Hal yumkinunī tawqīʿ ʿaqd al-ījār al-yawm?

The owner is very kind and helpful.
المالك لطيف جدًا ومفيد.
Al-mālik laṭīf jiddan wa mufīd.

I want to view the house before renting.
أريد رؤية المنزل قبل الاستئجار.
Urīdu ruʾyat al-manzil qabl al-istiʾjār.

The price is high; can we negotiate?
السعر مرتفع؛ هل يمكننا التفاوض؟
Al-siʿr murtafiʿ; hal yumkinunā al-tafāwuḍ?

Is there a laundry room in the apartment?
هل توجد غرفة غسيل في الشقة؟
Hal tūjad ghurfat ghasīl fī al-shaqqah?

I need a contract for six months.
أحتاج إلى عقد لمدة ستة أشهر.
Aḥtāju ilā ʿaqd limuddah sittah ashhur.

The house is close to the city center.
المنزل قريب من مركز المدينة.
Al-manzil qarīb min markaz al-madīnah.

Can I have the key after signing the contract?
هل يمكنني الحصول على المفتاح بعد توقيع العقد؟
Hal yumkinunī al-ḥuṣūl ʿalā al-miftāḥ baʿd tawqīʿ al-ʿaqd?

I don't like the location; it's too crowded.
لا يعجبني الموقع؛ إنه مزدحم جدًا.
Lā yuʿjibunī al-mawqiʿ; innahu muzdaḥim jiddan.

Chapter: 23

I went to the market yesterday.
ذهبت إلى السوق أمس.
Dhahabtu ilā al-sūq ams.

We studied English last year.
درسنا اللغة الإنجليزية العام الماضي.
Darasnā al-lughah al-Inglīziyyah al-ʿām al-māḍī.

He traveled to France last month.
سافر إلى فرنسا الشهر الماضي.
Sāfara ilā Faransā al-shahr al-māḍī.

She worked in a restaurant last summer.
عملت في مطعم الصيف الماضي.
ʿAmilat fī maṭʿam al-ṣayf al-māḍī.

I met my friends last week.
قابلت أصدقائي الأسبوع الماضي.
Qābaltu aṣdiqāʾī al-usbūʿ al-māḍī.

We ate at a new restaurant.
تناولنا الطعام في مطعم جديد.
Tanāwalnā al-ṭaʿām fī maṭʿam jadīd.

They played football in the park.
لعبوا كرة القدم في الحديقة.
Laʿibū kurat al-qadam fī al-ḥadīqah.

I watched a movie with my family.
شاهدت فيلمًا مع عائلتي.
Shāhadtu filmān maʿ ʿāʾilatī.

He saw a beautiful place in the city.
رأى مكانًا جميلًا في المدينة.
Raʾā makānan jamīlan fī al-madīnah.

I loved visiting my grandparents.
أحببت زيارة أجدادي.
Aḥbabtu ziyārat ajdādī.

She read a book about history.
قرأت كتابًا عن التاريخ.
Qaraʾat kitāban ʿan al-tārīkh.

We drank coffee in the morning.
شربنا القهوة في الصباح.
Sharibnā al-qahwah fī al-ṣabāḥ.

They bought gifts for their children.
اشتروا هدايا لأطفالهم.
Ishtarū hadāyā li-aṭfālihim.

I spent time with my cousin.
قضيت وقتًا مع ابن عمي.
Qaḍaytu waqtan maʿ ibn ʿammī.

We enjoyed our trip to the mountains.
استمتعنا برحلتنا إلى الجبال.
Istamtaʿnā bi-riḥlatinā ilā al-jibāl.

He did his homework before dinner.
قام بواجباته المنزلية قبل العشاء.
Qāma bi-wājibātih al-manziliyyah qabl al-ʿashāʾ.

She cooked dinner for the family.
طبخت العشاء للعائلة.
Ṭabakhat al-ʿashāʾ lil-ʿāʾilah.

I watched the sunset at the beach.
شاهدت غروب الشمس على الشاطئ.
Shāhadtu ghurūb al-shams ʿalā al-shāṭiʾ.

We visited the museum last weekend.
زرنا المتحف في نهاية الأسبوع الماضي.
Zurnā al-matḥaf fī nihāyat al-usbūʿ al-māḍī.

I studied Arabic when I was in school.
درست اللغة العربية عندما كنت في المدرسة.
Darastu al-lughah al-ʿArabiyyah ʿindamā kuntu fī al-madrasah.

Chapter: 24

I will study at the university next year.
سأدرس في الجامعة العام القادم.
Saʾadrusu fī al-jāmiʿah al-ʿām al-qādim.

We will travel to Italy next summer.
سنسافر إلى إيطاليا الصيف القادم.
Sanusāfir ilā Īṭāliyā al-ṣayf al-qādim.

She will learn French because she wants to work there.
ستتعلم الفرنسية لأنها تريد العمل هناك.
Satataʿallam al-faransiyyah liʾannaha turīd al-ʿamal hunāk.

I plan to buy a new car next month.
أخطط لشراء سيارة جديدة الشهر القادم.
Ukhattiṭ li-shirāʾ sayyārah jadīdah al-shahr al-qādim.

They will start their new jobs next week.
سيبدأون وظائفهم الجديدة الأسبوع القادم.
Sayabdaʾūn waẓāʾifihim al-jadīdah al-usbūʿ al-qādim.

I will be a doctor in the future.
سأكون طبيبًا في المستقبل.
Saʾakūn ṭabīban fī al-mustaqbal.

He will work in a big company soon.
سيعمل في شركة كبيرة قريبًا.
Sayʿamal fī sharikah kabīrah qarīban.

We will visit our grandparents next weekend.
سنزور أجدادنا نهاية الأسبوع القادم.
Sanzūr ajdādanā nihāyat al-usbūʿ al-qādim.

She will try to learn cooking this year.
ستحاول تعلم الطهي هذا العام.
Satuḥāwil taʿallum al-ṭahī hādhā al-ʿām.

I aspire to be an artist in the future.
أطمح أن أكون فنانًا في المستقبل.
Aṭmaḥ an akūn fannānan fī al-mustaqbal.

We want to live in a new house.
نريد أن نعيش في منزل جديد.
Nurīd an naʿīsh fī manzil jadīd.

I will go to the gym tomorrow.
سأذهب إلى الصالة الرياضية غدًا.
Saʾadhhab ilā al-ṣālah al-riyāḍiyyah ghadān.

He plans to start his own business next year.
يخطط لبدء مشروعه الخاص العام القادم.
Yukhaṭṭiṭ li-badʾ mashrūʿihi al-khāṣ al-ʿām al-qādim.

I will watch the new movie next Friday.
سأشاهد الفيلم الجديد يوم الجمعة القادمة.
Saʾushāhid al-film al-jadīd yawm al-jumʿah al-qādimah.

She will read a book this weekend.
ستقرأ كتابًا في نهاية هذا الأسبوع.
Sataqraʾ kitāban fī nihāyat hādhā al-usbūʿ.

We will meet our friends next Saturday.
سنلتقي بأصدقائنا يوم السبت القادم.
Sanaltaqī bi-aṣdiqāʾinā yawm al-sabt al-qādim.

I will try to learn a new skill next month.
سأحاول تعلم مهارة جديدة الشهر القادم.
Saʾuḥāwil taʿallum mahārah jadīdah al-shahr al-qādim.

He will travel to Japan next winter.
سيسافر إلى اليابان الشتاء القادم.
Sayusāfir ilā al-Yābān al-shitāʾ al-qādim.

I want to be fluent in Arabic.
أريد أن أكون طليقًا في اللغة العربية.
Urīd an akūn ṭalīqan fī al-lughah al-ʿArabiyyah.

We will go shopping next week.
سنذهب للتسوق الأسبوع القادم.
Sanadhhab li-tasawwuq al-usbūʿ al-qādim.

Chapter: 25

I want to study at the university.
أريد أن أدرس في الجامعة.
Urīd an adrus fī al-jāmiʿah.

My favorite subject is Science.
مادتي المفضلة هي العلوم.
Mādatī al-mufaḍḍalah hiya al-ʿulūm.

The teacher is very good and helpful.
المعلم جيد جدًا ومساعد.
Al-muʿallim jayid jiddan wa musāʿid.

I will do my homework after class.
سأقوم بواجباتي بعد الحصة.
Saʾaqūm bi-wājibātī baʿd al-ḥiṣṣah.

We have an exam next week.
لدينا امتحان الأسبوع القادم.
Ladaynā imtiḥān al-usbūʿ al-qādim.

I study at school every day.
أدرس في المدرسة كل يوم.
Adrus fī al-madrasah kull yawm.

My classmate is very friendly.
زميلي في الصف ودود جدًا.
Zamīlī fī al-ṣaff wadūd jiddan.

I want to get a degree in engineering.
أريد الحصول على درجة في الهندسة.
Urīd al-ḥuṣūl ʿalā darajah fī al-handasah.

The library is a quiet place for studying.
المكتبة مكان هادئ للدراسة.
Al-maktabah makān hādiʾ li-al-dirāsah.

I have a history exam tomorrow.
لدي امتحان تاريخ غدًا.
Ladayya imtiḥān tārīkh ghadān.

I plan to study abroad after graduation.
أخطط للدراسة في الخارج بعد التخرج.
Ukhaṭṭiṭ li-al-dirāsah fī al-khārij baʿd al-takharruj.

Our Math teacher is very strict.
معلم الرياضيات لدينا صارم جدًا.
Muʿallim al-riyāḍiyyāt ladaynā ṣārim jiddan.

I want to improve my Arabic language skills.
أريد تحسين مهاراتي في اللغة العربية.
Urīd taḥsīn mahārātī fī al-lughah al-ʿArabiyyah.

The classroom is big and bright.
الفصل كبير ومشرق.
Al-faṣl kabīr wa mushriq.

I have a dream to become a doctor.
لدي حلم أن أصبح طبيبًا.
Ladayya ḥulm an aṣbaḥ ṭabīban.

I need to prepare for my final exams.
أحتاج للتحضير لامتحاناتي النهائية.
Aḥtāj li-al-taḥḍīr li-imtiḥānātī al-nihāʾiyyah.

The school has a large library.
المدرسة لديها مكتبة كبيرة.
Al-madrasah ladayhā maktabah kabīrah.

I love my school because the teachers are great.
أحب مدرستي لأن المعلمين رائعون.
Uḥibb madrasatī liʾanna al-muʿallimīn rāʾiʿūn.

I need to review my lessons today.
أحتاج إلى مراجعة دروسي اليوم.
Aḥtāj ilā murājaʿat durūsī al-yawm.

My friend will study Science next semester.
صديقي سيدرس العلوم في الفصل الدراسي القادم.
Ṣadīqī sayadrus al-ʿulūm fī al-faṣl al-dirāsī al-qādim.

Chapter: 26

I want to go to the city center by bus.
أريد الذهاب إلى وسط المدينة بالحافلة.
Urīd al-dhahāb ilā wasaṭ al-madīnah bi-al-ḥāfilah.

The train is fast but sometimes crowded.
القطار سريع ولكنه مزدحم أحيانًا.
Al-qiṭār sarīʿ walākinahu muzdaḥim aḥyānan.

Where can I buy a ticket for the bus?
أين يمكنني شراء تذكرة للحافلة؟
Ayna yumkinunī shirāʾ tadhkirah li-al-ḥāfilah?

My flight departs from the airport at 8 AM.
رحلتي تنطلق من المطار الساعة الثامنة صباحًا.
Riḥlatī tantaṭliq min al-maṭār al-sāʿah al-thāminah ṣabāḥan.

The taxi is waiting at the hotel.
التاكسي ينتظر في الفندق.
Al-tāksī yantaẓir fī al-funduq.

How much is the ticket to the train station?
كم سعر التذكرة إلى محطة القطار؟
Kam siʿr al-tadhkirah ilā maḥaṭṭat al-qiṭār?

The bus stop is near my house.
موقف الحافلة قريب من منزلي.
Mawqif al-ḥāfilah qarīb min manzilī.

I prefer to ride a bicycle in the city.
أفضل ركوب الدراجة في المدينة.
Ufaddil rukūb al-darrājah fī al-madīnah.

The traffic is heavy during rush hour.
حركة المرور كثيفة خلال ساعة الذروة.
Ḥarakat al-murūr kathīfah khilāl sāʿat al-dhurwah.

Is the taxi expensive compared to the bus?
هل التاكسي مكلف مقارنة بالحافلة؟
Hal al-tāksī mukallif muqāranatan bi-al-ḥāfilah?

I usually take the car to work.
عادةً أذهب للعمل بالسيارة.
ʿĀdatan adhhab lil-ʿamal bi-al-sayyārah.

The bus arrives at the station at 6 PM.
تصل الحافلة إلى المحطة الساعة السادسة مساءً.
Taṣil al-ḥāfilah ilā al-maḥaṭṭah al-sāʿah al-sādisah masāʾan.

I need a map to find the train station.
أحتاج إلى خريطة للوصول إلى محطة القطار.
Aḥtāj ilā kharīṭah lil-wuṣūl ilā maḥaṭṭat al-qiṭār.

The driver is very polite and helpful.
السائق مهذب جدًا ومساعد.
Al-sāʾiq muʾaddab jiddan wa musāʿid.

We are walking to the restaurant tonight.
نحن نمشي إلى المطعم الليلة.
Naḥnu namshī ilā al-maṭʿam al-laylah.

The road to the airport is very busy.
الطريق إلى المطار مزدحم جدًا.
Al-ṭarīq ilā al-maṭār muzdaḥim jiddan.

How long does it take to get to the city center?
كم يستغرق الوصول إلى وسط المدينة؟
Kam yastaġriq al-wuṣūl ilā wasaṭ al-madīnah?

The motorcycle is faster than walking.
الدراجة النارية أسرع من المشي.
Al-darrājah al-nāriyyah asraʿ min al-mashī.

I like to travel by airplane for long distances.
أحب السفر بالطائرة للمسافات الطويلة.
Uḥibb al-safar bi-al-ṭāʾirah lil-masāfāt al-ṭawīlah.

The train leaves from platform number three.
القطار ينطلق من الرصيف رقم ثلاثة.
Al-qiṭār yanṭaliq min al-raṣīf raqam thalāthah.

Chapter: 27

We celebrate Eid with family and friends.
نحتفل بعيد الفطر مع العائلة والأصدقاء.
Naḥtafil bi-ʿīd al-fiṭr maʿa al-ʿāʾilah wa-al-aṣdiqāʾ.

The wedding will be on Sunday evening.
سيكون الزفاف مساء يوم الأحد.
Sayakūn al-zifāf masāʾ yawm al-aḥad.

My birthday is in the summer.
عيد ميلادي في الصيف.
ʿĪd mīlādi fī al-ṣayf.

Traditional clothes are worn during festivals.
تُلبس الملابس التقليدية خلال المهرجانات.
Tulbas al-malābis al-taqlīdiyyah khilāl al-mahrajānāt.

The cultural festival had delicious food and music.
كان المهرجان الثقافي يحتوي على طعام لذيذ وموسيقى.
Kāna al-mahrajān al-thaqāfī yaḥtawī ʿalā ṭaʿām ladhīdh wa-mūsīqā.

Congratulations on your new job!
مبروك على وظيفتك الجديدة!
Mabrūk ʿalā waẓīfatak al-jadīdah!

We visited our relatives during the holiday.
زرنا أقاربنا خلال العطلة.
Zurnā aqāribnā khilāl al-ʿuṭlah.

The decorations at the party were beautiful.
كانت الزينة في الحفلة جميلة.
Kānat al-zīnah fī al-ḥaflah jamīlah.

I received a gift from my friend.
تلقيت هدية من صديقي.
Talaqqaytu hadiyyah min ṣadīqī.

Do you like traditional celebrations?
هل تحب الاحتفالات التقليدية؟
Hal tuḥibb al-iḥtifālāt al-taqlīdiyyah?

The guest brought a lovely gift to the house.
جلب الضيف هدية جميلة إلى المنزل.
Jalaba al-ḍayf hadiyyah jamīlah ilā al-manzil.

The family gathered for a large feast.
تجمعَت العائلة لتناول وليمة كبيرة.
Tajammaʿat al-ʿāʾilah li-tanāwul walīmah kabīrah.

Ramadan is a month of fasting and prayer.
رمضان هو شهر الصيام والصلاة.
Ramaḍān huwa shahr al-ṣiyām wa-al-ṣalāh.

We light candles during the celebration.
نضيء الشموع خلال الاحتفال.
Nuḍīʾ al-shumūʿ khilāl al-iḥtifāl.

The holiday traditions are very important to us.
تقاليد العطلات مهمة جدًا بالنسبة لنا.
Taqālīd al-ʿuṭalāt muhimmah jiddan binisbatan lanā.

The wedding had many traditional rituals.
كان في الزفاف العديد من الطقوس التقليدية.
Kāna fī al-zifāf al-ʿadīd min al-ṭuqūs al-taqlīdiyyah.

I sent an invitation to all my friends.
أرسلت دعوة لجميع أصدقائي.
Arsaltu daʿwah li-jamīʿ aṣdiqāʾī.

The food at the festival was amazing.
كان الطعام في المهرجان رائعًا.
Kāna al-ṭaʿām fī al-mahrajān rāʾiʿan.

I enjoy learning about different cultures.
أستمتع بتعلم الثقافات المختلفة.
Astamti' bi-ta'allum al-thaqāfāt al-mukhtalifah.

The party starts at 7 PM on Friday.
تبدأ الحفلة الساعة السابعة مساء يوم الجمعة.
Tabda' al-ḥaflah al-sā'ah al-sābi'ah masā' yawm al-jum'ah.

Chapter: 28

We need to schedule a meeting with the manager.
نحتاج إلى تحديد اجتماع مع المدير.
Naḥtāj ilā taḥdīd ijtimā' ma'a al-mudīr.

The company is launching a new product next month.
ستطلق الشركة منتجًا جديدًا الشهر القادم.
Satutliq al-sharikah muntajan jadīdan al-shahr al-qādim.

The employee is preparing a report on the project.
الموظف يحضر تقريرًا عن المشروع.
Al-muwaẓẓaf yuḥaḍḍir taqrīran 'an al-mashrū'.

We have a meeting with the client tomorrow.
لدينا اجتماع مع العميل غدًا.
Ladanā ijtimā' ma'a al-'amīl ghadan.

The contract needs to be signed before the deadline.
العقد يحتاج إلى توقيع قبل الموعد النهائي.
Al-'aqd yaḥtāj ilā tawqī' qabla al-maw'id al-nihā'ī.

The team is working on the new marketing plan.
الفريق يعمل على الخطة التسويقية الجديدة.
Al-farīq ya'mal 'alā al-khiṭṭah al-taswīqiyyah al-jadīdah.

Our goal is to increase sales by 20%.
هدفنا هو زيادة المبيعات بنسبة 20%.
Hadafunā huwa ziyādat al-mabī'āt binisbat 20%.

The manager will present the project to the team.
سيقدم المدير المشروع للفريق.
Sayuqaddim al-mudīr al-mashrūʿ lil-farīq.

The budget for this plan needs to be reviewed.
الميزانية لهذه الخطة تحتاج إلى مراجعة.
Al-mīzāniyyah li-hādhihi al-khiṭṭah taḥtāj ilā murājaʿah.

We will discuss the details of the contract today.
سنناقش تفاصيل العقد اليوم.
Sanunāqish tafāṣīl al-ʿaqd al-yawm.

The company is looking for a new employee.
الشركة تبحث عن موظف جديد.
Al-sharikah tabḥath ʿan muwaẓẓaf jadīd.

The salary for this position is very competitive.
الراتب لهذا المنصب تنافسي جدًا.
Al-rātib li-hādhā al-manṣib tanāfusī jiddan.

Our team is collaborating on this project.
فريقنا يتعاون في هذا المشروع.
Farīqunā yataʿāwan fī hādhā al-mashrūʿ.

The client agreed to the terms of the agreement.
وافق العميل على شروط الاتفاقية.
Wāfaq al-ʿamīl ʿalā shurūṭ al-ittifāqiyyah.

We have a deadline to complete this task.
لدينا موعد نهائي لإنهاء هذه المهمة.
Ladanā mawʿid nihāʾī li-ʾinhāʾ hādhihi al-muhimmah.

The business proposal will be presented next week.
سيتم تقديم العرض التجاري الأسبوع القادم.
Sayatimm taqdīm al-ʿarḍ al-tijāri al-usbūʿ al-qādim.

The supplier is providing the materials for the project.
المورد يوفر المواد للمشروع.
Al-muwarrid yuwaffir al-mawād lil-mashrūʿ.

The employee is responsible for the sales report.
الموظف مسؤول عن تقرير المبيعات.
Al-muwaẓẓaf masʾūl ʿan taqrīr al-mabīʿāt.

We need to arrange an appointment with the client.
نحتاج إلى ترتيب موعد مع العميل.
Naḥtāj ilā tartīb mawʿid maʿa al-ʿamīl.

The manager is reviewing the budget for the project.
المدير يراجع الميزانية للمشروع.
Al-mudīr yurājiʿ al-mīzāniyyah lil-mashrūʿ.

Chapter: 29

I have a problem with the service; it's unacceptable.
لدي مشكلة مع الخدمة؛ إنها غير مقبولة.
Ladaya mushkilah maʿa al-khidmah; innahā ghayru maqbūlah.

The air conditioner is not working; it needs repair.
مكيف الهواء لا يعمل؛ يحتاج إلى إصلاح.
Mukayyif al-hawāʾ lā yaʿmal; yaḥtāj ilā iṣlāḥ.

The product is defective; I want a refund.
المنتج معيب؛ أريد استرداد المبلغ.
Al-muntaj maʿīb; urīd istirdād al-mablagh.

There is a mistake in the bill; can you check it?
هناك خطأ في الفاتورة؛ هل يمكنك التحقق منها؟
Hunāka khatāʾ fī al-fātūrah; hal yumkinuka al-taḥaqqaq minhā?

I am not satisfied with the quality of the food.
أنا غير راضٍ عن جودة الطعام.
Anā ghayru rāḍin ʿan jawdat al-ṭaʿām.

There was a delay in my order, and I am unhappy.
كان هناك تأخير في طلبي، وأنا غير سعيد.
Kāna hunāka taʾkhīr fī ṭalabī, wa-anā ghayru saʿīd.

Can I file a complaint about the poor service?
هل يمكنني تقديم شكوى عن الخدمة السيئة؟
Hal yumkinunī taqdīm shakwā ʿan al-khidmah al-sayyiʾah?

I would like to talk to the manager about the problem.
أود التحدث إلى المدير حول المشكلة.
Awaddu al-taḥadduth ilā al-mudīr ḥawla al-mushkilah.

The technician came but didn't fix the issue.
جاء الفني لكنه لم يصلح المشكلة.
Jā'a al-fannī lakinnahu lam yuṣliḥ al-mushkilah.

I need compensation for the delay in service.
أحتاج إلى تعويض عن التأخير في الخدمة.
Aḥtāj ilā taʿwīḍ ʿan al-taʾkhīr fī al-khidmah.

The room is not clean; this is a big problem.
الغرفة ليست نظيفة؛ هذه مشكلة كبيرة.
Al-ghurfah laysa naẓīfah; hādhih mushkilah kabīrah.

We are not satisfied with the agreement terms.
نحن غير راضين عن شروط الاتفاق.
Naḥnu ghayru rāḍīn ʿan shurūṭ al-ittiqāq.

I want to return this item because it's not suitable.
أريد إعادة هذا العنصر لأنه غير مناسب.
Urīd iʿādah hādhā al-ʿunsur li-annahu ghayru munāsib.

There is a technical problem with the system.
هناك مشكلة فنية في النظام.
Hunāka mushkilah fanniyyah fī al-niẓām.

We need to report this issue to customer service.
نحتاج إلى الإبلاغ عن هذه المشكلة إلى خدمة العملاء.
Naḥtāj ilā al-iblāgh ʿan hādhih al-mushkilah ilā khidmat al-ʿumlāʾ.

My flight was postponed; I need to complain.
تم تأجيل رحلتي؛ أحتاج إلى الشكوى.
Tam taʾjīl raḥlatī; aḥtāj ilā al-shakwā.

The food is cold, and the service is slow.
الطعام بارد، والخدمة بطيئة.
Al-ṭaʿām bārid, wa al-khidmah baṭīʾah.

I received the wrong order; please fix this mistake.
تلقيت الطلب الخاطئ؛ يرجى تصحيح هذا الخطأ.
Talaqqayt al-ṭalab al-khāṭiʾ; yurjā taṣḥīḥ hādhā al-khaṭā.

Can I speak to someone about this issue?
هل يمكنني التحدث إلى شخص ما حول هذه المشكلة؟
Hal yumkinunī al-taḥadduth ilā shaḵṣ mā ḥawla hādhih al-mushkilah?

The technician was late, and the problem is still there.
تأخر الفني، والمشكلة لا تزال قائمة.
Taʾakhkhar al-fannī, wa al-mushkilah lā tathāl qā'imah.

Chapter: 30

I am proud of my progress this year.
أنا فخور بتقدمي هذا العام.
Anā fakhūr bi-taqaddumī hādhā al-ʿām.

Our team achieved great success in the project.
حقق فريقنا نجاحًا كبيرًا في المشروع.
Ḥaqqaq farīqnā najāḥan kabīran fī al-mashrūʿ.

We should celebrate our accomplishments together.
يجب أن نحتفل بإنجازاتنا معًا.
Yajibu an naḥtafil bi-injāzātinā maʿan.

Your determination helped you overcome challenges.
عزيمتك ساعدتك على التغلب على التحديات.
ʿAzīmatuka sāʿadatuka ʿalā al-taghallub ʿalā al-taḥaddiyāt.

I want to improve my skills in the future.
أريد تحسين مهاراتي في المستقبل.
Urīd taḥsīn mahārātī fī al-mustaqbal.

We set our goals and achieved them with effort.
وضعنا أهدافنا وحققناها بالجهد.
Waḍaʿnā ahdāfnā wa ḥaqqaqnāhā bil-juhd.

Thank you for your support; it made a big difference.
شكرًا لدعمك؛ لقد أحدث فرقًا كبيرًا.
Shukran li-daʿmika; laqad aḥdatha farqan kabīran.

We are celebrating the victory of our hard work.
نحن نحتفل بنجاح عملنا الجاد.
Naḥnu naḥtafil bi-najāḥ ʿamalinā al-jād.

Reflecting on our journey, we have come a long way.
عند التأمل في رحلتنا، قطعنا شوطًا طويلًا.
ʿInda al-taʾammul fī riḥlatinā, qaṭaʿnā shawṭan ṭawīlan.

The team's success is a result of joint efforts.
نجاح الفريق هو نتيجة للجهود المشتركة.
Najāḥ al-farīq huwa natījah lil-juhūd al-mushtarakah.

I have learned a lot from this experience.
لقد تعلمت الكثير من هذه التجربة.
Laqad taʿallamtu al-kathīr min hādhih al-tajrubah.

Let's look forward to achieving more in the future.
دعنا نتطلع لتحقيق المزيد في المستقبل.
Daʿnā nattaliʿ li-taḥqīq al-mazeed fī al-mustaqbal.

Your progress this year is outstanding.
تقدمك هذا العام متميز.
Taqaddumuka hādhā al-ʿām mutamayiz.

We faced challenges but kept moving forward.
واجهنا التحديات لكننا استمرينا في التقدم.
Wājahnā al-taḥaddiyāt lakinnā istamaraynā fī al-taqaddum.

Celebrating progress is as important as making it.
الاحتفال بالتقدم مهم بقدر تحقيقه.
Al-iḥtifāl bi-al-taqaddum muhim bi-qadr taḥqīqih.

This is a big step towards our future goals.
هذه خطوة كبيرة نحو أهدافنا المستقبلية.
Hādhih khuṭwah kabīrah naḥw ahdāfnā al-mustaqbaliyyah.

Your efforts are truly appreciated by everyone.
جهودك مقدرة حقًا من قبل الجميع.
Juhūdika muqaddarah ḥaqqan min qibal al-jamī'.

Keep aiming high; your ambition will lead you to success.
استمر في الطموح العالي؛ طموحك سيقودك إلى النجاح.
Istamirr fī al-ṭamūḥ al-'ālī; ṭamūḥuka sayuqūduka ilā al-najāḥ.

Reviewing our achievements shows how far we've come.
مراجعة إنجازاتنا تُظهر مدى تقدمنا.
Murāja'at injāzātinā tuẓhir madā taqaddumnā.

We are on the right path to greater accomplishments.
نحن على الطريق الصحيح نحو إنجازات أكبر.
Naḥnu 'alā al-ṭarīq al-ṣaḥīḥ naḥw injāzāt akbar.

Arabic Alphabet Forms

Letter Name	Isolated	Initial	Medial	Final
أ (Alif)	أ	أ	ـا	ـا
ب (Ba)	ب	بـ	ـبـ	ـب
ت (Ta)	ت	تـ	ـتـ	ـت
ث (Sa)	ث	ثـ	ـثـ	ـث
ج (Jeem)	ج	جـ	ـجـ	ـج
ح (Ha)	ح	حـ	ـحـ	ـح
خ (Kha)	خ	خـ	ـخـ	ـخ
د (Dal)	د	د	ـد	ـد
ذ (Dhal)	ذ	ذ	ـذ	ـذ
ر (Ra)	ر	ر	ـر	ـر
ز (Za)	ز	ز	ـز	ـز
س (Seen)	س	سـ	ـسـ	ـس
ش (Sheen)	ش	شـ	ـشـ	ـش
ص (Sad)	ص	صـ	ـصـ	ـص
ض (Zad)	ض	ضـ	ـضـ	ـض
ط (Ta)	ط	طـ	ـطـ	ـط
ظ (Za)	ظ	ظـ	ـظـ	ـظ
ع (Ain)	ع	عـ	ـعـ	ـع
غ (Ghain)	غ	غـ	ـغـ	ـغ
ف (Fa)	ف	فـ	ـفـ	ـف
ق (Qaf)	ق	قـ	ـقـ	ـق
ك (Kaf)	ك	كـ	ـكـ	ـك
ل (Lam)	ل	لـ	ـلـ	ـل
م (Meem)	م	مـ	ـمـ	ـم
ن (Noon)	ن	نـ	ـنـ	ـن
ه (Ha)	هـ	هـ	ـهـ	ـه
و (Waw)	و	و	ـو	ـو
ي (Ya)	ي	يـ	ـيـ	ـي

Symbols of Arabic (Harakat)

Fat-ha	Above the letter	بَ	ba
Kas-ra	Below the letter	بِ	bi
Dam-ma	Above the letter	بُ	bu
Double Fat-ha	Above the letter	بً	ban
Double Kas-ra	Below the letter	بٍ	bin
Double Dam-ma	Above the letter	بٌ	bun
Sukoon	Above the letter	بْ	b (no vowel sound)
Shadda	Above the letter	بّ	double sound

www.ingramcontent.com/pod-product-compliance
Lightning Source LLC
Chambersburg PA
CBHW052149220526
45471CB00004B/1594
9798340604774